Landmarks of world li

Shakespeare

H

Landmarks of world literature

General Editor: J. P. Stern

SHAKESPEARE

Hamlet

PAUL A. CANTOR

University of Virginia

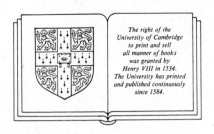

The right of the
University of Cambridge
to print and sell
all manner of books
was granted by
Henry VIII in 1534.
The University has printed
and published continuously
since 1584.

CAMBRIDGE UNIVERSITY PRESS

Cambridge
New York   New Rochelle
Melbourne   Sydney

Published by the Press Syndicate of the University of Cambridge
The Pitt Building, Trumpington Street, Cambridge CB2 1RP
32 East 57th Street, New York, NY 10022, USA
10 Stamford Road, Oakleigh, Melbourne 3166, Australia

First published 1989

Printed in Great Britain at the University Press, Cambridge

British Library cataloguing in publication data
Cantor, Paul A. (Paul Arthur)
Shakespeare, Hamlet − (Landmarks of
world literature)
1. Drama in English. Shakespeare, William,
1564–1616. Hamlet − Critical studies
I. Title   II. Series
822.3′3

Library of Congress cataloging in publication data
Cantor, Paul A. (Paul Arthur), 1945–
Shakespeare, Hamlet / Paul A. Cantor.
      p.   cm. − (Landmarks of world literature)
Bibliography.
ISBN 0–521–34190–6. − ISBN 0–521–34983–4 (pbk.)
1. Shakespeare, William, 1564–161. Hamlet. I. Title.
II. Series.
PR2807.C25   1989
822.3′3 − dc 19   88–34127   CIP

ISBN 0 521 34190 6 hard covers
ISBN 0 521 34983 4 paperback

GG

What a work this *Hamlet* is! The interest in it, lasting over centuries, probably arose from the fact that a new type, fully developed, stands out as totally estranged in a mediaeval environment that has remained totally unmodified. The scream for revenge, ennobled by the Greek tragedians, then ruled out by Christianity, in the drama of *Hamlet* is still loud enough . . . to make the new doubting, testing, planning appear in a strange light.

Bertolt Brecht

Skepticism . . . always develops when races or classes . . . are crossed suddenly and decisively. In the new generation that, as it were, has inherited in its blood diverse standards and values, everything is unrest, disturbance, doubt, attempt; the best forces have an inhibiting effect, the very virtues do not allow each other to grow and become strong; balance, a center of gravity, and perpendicular poise are lacking in body and soul. But what becomes sickest and degenerates most in such hybrids is the *will*; they no longer know independence of decisions and the intrepid sense of pleasure in willing — they doubt the 'freedom of the will' even in their dreams.

Friedrich Nietzsche, Beyond Good and Evil

Contents

Preface

I would have hesitated to add another book to the vast literature on *Hamlet* if the conception of this series had not offered an opportunity to take a fresh look at the play by considering it in the context of world literature. Accordingly, my discussion ranges from Homer to Tom Stoppard. I believe that our understanding of *Hamlet* can benefit from this kind of wide-angled approach: it seems to be uniquely situated at the intersection of ancient and modern literature. On the one hand, Hamlet strikes us as the most modern of Shakespeare's heroes, caught up in a kind of questioning and doubt that seems all-too-familiar to us in the twentieth century. On the other hand, the story of Hamlet has its roots in the most primitive strata of the imagination, a tale of blood feuds and vengeance, the kind of legend found at the fountainhead of many of the great literatures of the west, including Greek and Norse. Thus *Hamlet* has a peculiarly rich texture: it has passages that sound as though they could have come from an Elizabethan translation of the *Iliad*, but at other times the dialogue seems to anticipate a work like *Waiting for Godot*. Recognition of this hybrid character of *Hamlet* provides a profound clue to the sort of questions Shakespeare is exploring in the play.

Although I have tried to provide as comprehensive a discussion of *Hamlet* as a brief book will allow, I have chosen to focus on the issue of heroism in the play, specifically on the way Hamlet stands poised between an older and a newer conception of heroism, between one view which sees heroism as something external – triumphing physically over an opponent – and another view which sees heroism as something internal – a quality of soul which cannot always be manifested in deeds. I realise that talking about heroism in Shakespeare's plays is unfashionable at the moment, since for a variety of reasons, heroism has come to be viewed as a deeply problematic notion. I believe that the anti-heroic tendency of much contemporary criticism is causing us to lose sight of Shakespeare's tragic vision, but in any case, I will be arguing that what makes Hamlet unique as a hero is precisely the fact that heroism has become problematic for him, and yet he can still respond to a heroic model (though obviously not in a simple way). Shakespeare's historical situation facilitated a comprehensiveness of vision when he approached the issue of heroism, and thus a play like *Hamlet* can help to re-open it for us. Living in the Renaissance, Shakespeare was still in touch with classical conceptions of heroism, but he was also aware of how those notions were being challenged by newer conceptions, particularly under the influence of Christianity. Thus I begin my discussion of *Hamlet* with an attempt to survey the Renaissance context in which Shakespeare created the play.

In analysing heroism and tragedy in *Hamlet*, I have drawn heavily upon Hegel and Nietzsche. Since both discuss *Hamlet* in some detail – Hegel in his *Aesthetics* and Nietzsche in *The Birth of Tragedy* – I should explain that, while I make use of their general ideas, I disagree with them when they interpret this specific play. Though a volume such as this does not offer the opportunity to work out one's differences with critics at length, I will say that in my view both Hegel and Nietzsche failed to see how powerfully their ideas could illuminate *Hamlet* because they approached it within a tradition of interpretation that grew out of Romanticism (see the first section of chapter 2). Both saw the problem of Hamlet as somehow rooted in his individual soul, whereas I will be arguing that the conflicts within Hamlet mirror a more fundamental tension in the Renaissance culture in which he lives. Thus, although the conflicts in *Hamlet* are not objectified in institutions such as the family or the state, they are not merely subjective in Hegel's terms either. I could in fact formulate my argument in Hegelian terms by stating that *Hamlet* lies as it were halfway between ancient and modern tragedy as Hegel conceives them (whereas he himself views the play as a purely modern tragedy).

All my quotations and line citations from Shakespeare are drawn from G. Blakemore Evans's edition, *The Riverside Shakespeare* (Boston, 1974). In my quotations from *Hamlet*, I have occasionally altered Evans's spelling, and at one point his wording (in Hamlet's first soliloquy, I prefer the Folio reading of *solid* at I.ii.129 over the Second Quarto reading of *sallied*, changed to *sullied* by many modern editors). As is often the case in Shakespeare, the textual situation in *Hamlet* is complex; readers interested in the details should consult any scholarly edition such as Evans's. Suffice it to say here that we are faced with two authoritative texts of the play, the Second Quarto and the First Folio, which largely overlap but also diverge at many points. Though most editors use the Second Quarto text as the basis for their editions, it cannot simply be preferred to the Folio text (which for one thing contains some 90 lines not found in the Second Quarto). I do not have space to go into the issue here, but I will say that, although the uncertainty about the text of *Hamlet* is troubling and should be borne in mind in any analysis, I do not believe that we are dealing with two distinct versions of the play or that questions about the text need materially affect our interpretation of the play as a whole.

Bearing in mind Hamlet's remark, 'Beggar that I am, I am even poor in thanks' (II.ii.272), I would like to acknowledge the help of the following people over the years in working out my interpretation of *Hamlet* and in the writing of this specific book: Barbara Black, Gordon Braden, Douglas Hoffman, Daniel Kinney, Stuart Kurland, Michael Moses, Thomas Peyser, and James M. Wood.

Chronology

Shakespeare's life and works | *Historical and cultural events*

1558		Elizabeth becomes Queen of England
1561		Francis Bacon born
1562		Lope de Vega born; Norton and Sackville: *Gorboduc* (first English blank verse tragedy)
1563		Thirty-Nine Articles of the Anglican Church; John Dowland born
1564	Shakespeare born in Stratford (Christened 26 April)	Galileo and Christopher Marlowe born; Michelangelo dies
1566		James VI of Scotland born
1567		James becomes king; Claudio Monteverdi born; Palestrina: *Missa Papae Marcelli*
1571		Battle of Lepanto
1572		St. Bartholomew's Day Massacre; Peace of Constantinople; John Donne born; Camoens: *Lusiads*
1573		Ben Jonson born
1575		Tasso: *Gerusalemme Liberata*; Tallis and Byrd: *Cantiones Sacrae*

1576		Building of The Theatre, first permanent playhouse in London
1579		North's translation of Plutarch's *Lives*
1580		Sir Francis Drake completes circumnavigation of globe
1582	Marries Anne Hathaway; licence issued 27 November	
1583	Daughter born; christened Susanna 26 May	
1585	Twin son and daughter born; christened Hamnet and Judith 2 February	Colonists sent to Roanoke Island, Virginia; Cardinal Richelieu and Heinrich Schütz born; Thomas Tallis dies
1586	Around this time, seems to have left Stratford	
1587		Mary, Queen of Scots, executed; Kyd: *The Spanish Tragedy* (?); Marlowe: *1 Tamburlaine*
1588		Spanish Armada defeated; Marlowe: *2 Tamburlaine* born; Thomas Hobbes
1589	Seems to have begun writing plays and acting in London; *1 Henry VI* may have been his first play	Kyd: *Hamlet* (?)
1590		James VI marries Anne of Denmark; Spenser: *Faerie Queene*, Books I–III
1591		Sidney: *Astrophel and Stella*
1593	*Venus and Adonis*	Marlowe dies; Sidney: *Arcadia*

Year	Shakespeare	Events
1594	*The Rape of Lucrece*	Lord Chamberlain's Men formed (Shakespeare's theatre company); Palestrina dies
1595	First associated with Lord Chamberlain's Men	Byrd: *Mass for 5 Voices*
1596	Son (Hamnet) dies	René Descartes born; Spenser: *Faerie Queene*, Books I–VI
1597	Buys New Place in Stratford	1st Edition of Bacon's *Essays*; Dowland: *First Book of Songes*
1598		Edict of Nantes; Philip II of Spain dies; Boris Godunov becomes Czar; first instalment of George Chapman's translation of Homer
1599	*Henry V; Julius Caesar*	The Globe Theatre opens; Essex's expedition to Ireland; Spenser dies; Oliver Cromwell born
1600	*Hamlet* written and performed (?)	East India Company formed; Giordano Bruno burned at Rome; Calderón born; Peri: *Euridice* (first opera)
1601	Father (John) dies	Insurrection and execution of Essex; Siege of Ostend; London War of the Theatres
1603	First Quarto of *Hamlet* published	Queen Elizabeth dies; James VI becomes James I of England; Chamberlain's Men become King's Men; Florio's translation of Montaigne's *Essays*
1604	*Othello*; Second Quarto of *Hamlet* published	Treaty of Peace between Spain and England; Dowland: *Lachrymae*

1605	*King Lear*	Gunpowder Plot; Bacon: *Advancement of Learning*; Cervantes: *Don Quixote*, Pt. I
1606	*Macbeth*	Rembrandt and Corneille born
1607	Susanna Shakespeare marries Dr. John Hall	Jamestown, Virginia settlement; Monteverdi: *Orfeo*
1608	Becomes shareholder in Second Blackfriars Theatre; Mother (Mary) dies	John Milton born
1609	Pirated edition of Shakespeare's *Sonnets*	
1610	May have returned to Stratford	Monteverdi: *Vespers*; Galileo: *The Starry Messenger*
1611	*The Tempest*	King James Version of the Bible
1612		Giovanni Gabrieli dies
1613	*Henry VIII*, with John Fletcher (?), possibly his last literary effort	Globe Theatre burns down during performance of *Henry VIII*; Bacon made Attorney-General; Galileo: *Letters on Sunspots*
1614		Globe Theatre rebuilt; Raleigh: *History of the World*
1615		Cervantes: *Don Quixote*, Pt. II
1616	Dies (23 April); buried 25 April in Stratford; Judith Shakespeare marries Thomas Quiney	Cervantes dies; Bacon made Lord Chancellor; Jonson: *Works*
1623	First Folio published	William Byrd dies; Pascal born; Galileo: *The Assayer*

Chapter 1

Hamlet and the Renaissance

The Renaissance context

Ever since nineteenth-century historians such as Jules Michelet and Jacob Burckhardt began elaborating a systematic concept of the Renaissance, the idea has proved controversial. Some have questioned whether it is accurate to speak of the Renaissance as a distinct period; others have confined themselves to questioning the dating of the age, or proposing a variety of Renaissances. Certainly when one surveys what has come to be known as the Renaissance, it looks different in different countries, and seems to proceed at different rates in different areas (the Renaissance in painting, for example, occurred long before what we think of as the Renaissance in music). Nevertheless, the fact that one still speaks of 'Renaissances' in these cases suggests some kind of underlying unity to the phenomena. And many of the figures who fall into the period we label the Renaissance show signs of having conceived of themselves as living in a distinct era, with a strong sense of having broken with the past. Though they may not have used the term 'Renaissance', writers such as Francis Bacon in his *The Advancement of Learning* (1605) speak of themselves as coming at the dawn of a new age. In the end, although one must grant that the idea of the Renaissance is the construction of historians, the concept remains useful for understanding a wide range of phenomena, including, as I hope to show, Shakespeare's achievement in *Hamlet*.

The Renaissance, as the name implies, was a rebirth: the rebirth of classical antiquity in the modern world, beginning in Italy roughly in the fourteenth and fifteenth centuries and gradually spreading to the rest of Europe. Today we tend to think of the age largely in aesthetic terms, and point to such phenomena as the imitation of Greek sculpture and architecture, the attempts to recapture the spirit of Homer and Virgil in epic, or the effort to recreate Greek tragedy in the modern form of opera. But the Renaissance was not merely what we would call a cultural event. It reached far deeper into the fabric of European life, involving attempts to revive the political forms of classical antiquity as well as the artistic. One can see this in the imperial ambitions of many Renaissance states, their hopes to rival Rome's conquests, reflected, for example, in Edmund Spenser's conception of England following Rome as the third Troy. More importantly, in Renaissance Italy attempts were made to revive the republican forms of government which were characteristic of the ancient world and which had largely disappeared during the Middle Ages. Indeed it is no accident that the Renaissance began in Italy, where republics such as Florence and Venice came closer than any other communities in Europe to recreating the civic life which had provided the basis for the great cultural achievements of Athens and Rome.

But the Renaissance was not simply a return to the principles or conditions of the ancient world. It was a rebirth of classical antiquity within a Christian culture, and that made a complete return to the way of life of pagan Greece and Rome impossible. As a result, the era was characterised by an uneasy and unstable alliance of classical and Christian elements. To be sure, there are ways in which classical and Christian culture can be harmonised. The ethics of both Christianity and classical philosophy tend to denigrate the passions as the animal part of human nature and to view the control of them as the goal of ethical conduct. Plato's presentation of philosophy as preparation for dying in the *Phaedo* could easily be reinterpreted in Christian terms; a character in Erasmus's colloquy, 'The Religious Banquet' (1533), when he reads Socrates' last words, feels moved to say: 'Sancte Socrates, ora pro nobis' (254; 'Saint Socrates, pray for us').

Renaissance thinkers could draw upon a long tradition of adopting classical writings to Christian purposes. Even in the Middle Ages, many classical authors were viewed as anticipating Christian truths and were virtually canonised in the process. Virgil's Fourth Eclogue, with its prophecy of a new-born child who will usher in a golden age of peace, was long seen as reflecting a dim pagan awareness of the coming of Christ.

Such examples of the reconciliation of classical authors with Christian doctrine have led many historians to view the Renaissance as a grand and successful synthesis of classicism and Christianity, usually discussed under the label 'Christian humanism'. This term has in fact become so much a part of discourse on the Renaissance that we are in danger of forgetting that it is almost as much of an oxymoron as Romeo's 'cold fire' or 'sick health' (I.i.181). Christianity is not a form of humanism in any ordinary sense of the term; indeed throughout most of its history Christianity has been the antithesis of humanism. Thus, although one can certainly find authors in the Renaissance who thought of themselves as Christian humanists, one must remember that their programme was viewed as controversial at the time, and often seen, in fact, as heretical by church authorities. Any investigation of the phenomenon ought to begin with a frank admission of how deeply problematic the concept is, of how many tensions and contradictions lie concealed beneath what appears to be a simple label. Discussions of Christian humanism often make it seem as if nothing could be easier than to synthesise Christianity and classicism. But in fact the two traditions have almost always been antagonists, if not mortal enemies. Christianity arose in conscious opposition to classical values; classical culture in the form of Rome long sought to stamp out Christianity; though the two traditions have at times appeared to make their peace with each other, their reconciliations have been more like temporary truces than lasting alliances, and eventually one has always tried to triumph over the other.

One can see how difficult it is to fuse Christianity and

classicism if one looks at the concept of heroism in the two traditions. The Achilles of Homer's *Iliad* is the classical hero *par excellence*, and it would be hard to imagine a less Christian figure. Achilles is proud, aggressive, vengeful, exulting in his power, and implacable in his enmity. Consider how he characteristically boasts of his triumph over Hector and humiliates his fallen victim:

> Hektor, surely you thought as you killed Patroklos you would be
> safe, and since I was far away you thought nothing of me,
> o fool, for an avenger was left, far greater than he was,
> behind him and away by the hollow ships. And it was I;
> and I have broken your strength; on you the dogs and the vultures
> shall feed and foully rip you; the Achaians will bury
>   Patroklos . . .
> No more entreaty of me, you dog, by knees or parents.
> I wish only that my spirit and fury would drive me
> to hack your meat away and eat it raw for the things that
> you have done to me.   (XXII, 331–6, 345–8)

This is admittedly an extreme moment for Achilles, and even within the *Iliad* he has to learn to moderate his anger. Moreover, the Achillean model did not go unchallenged within Greek culture, as one can see if one looks at Socrates' critique of Homer in Plato's *Republic* (which suggests why the classical philosophic tradition was more easily reconciled with Christianity than the classical heroic tradition). But when all these qualifications are made, the fact remains that Achilles in all his pride and rage was held up as a model to Greek youth; Homer's portrait supposedly helped to fire the ambitions of Alexander the Great. The centrality of Achilles as hero within classical culture tells us something about the ancient Greeks (and Romans as well): the way they prized the whole spirited side of human nature – what the Greeks called *thumos* – the complex of pride, anger, indignation and ambition which fuelled the deeds of the great classical heroes (in fact as well as in fiction).

Contrast Achilles' speech with the words of the central model of the Christian tradition, Jesus himself, in his Sermon on the Mount:

Blessed are the poor in spirit: for theirs is the kingdom of
heaven . . .
Blessed are the meek: for they shall inherit the earth . . .
Blessed are the merciful: for they shall obtain mercy . . .
But I say unto you, That whosoever is angry with his
brother without a cause shall be in danger of the judgement:
but whosoever shall say, Thou fool, shall be in danger of
hell fire . . .
Ye have heard that it hath been said, An eye for an eye, and
a tooth for a tooth:
But I say unto you, That ye resist not evil: but whosoever
shall smite thee on thy right cheek, turn to him the other also.
                (Matthew 5: 3, 7, 9, 22, 38–9; Authorised Version)

Judged by these principles, Achilles is headed straight for
hell. Jesus is in every respect the antithesis of the classical
hero: he is humble rather than proud, merciful rather than
vengeful, passive rather than aggressive, and forgiving of sins
rather than unyielding in hatred. In classical terms, one might
question whether there is in fact anything heroic at all about
Jesus, but the tendency of Christianity is to redefine heroism
so that suffering misery becomes a higher or deeper form
of heroism than inflicting misery. The Christian hero *par
excellence* is the martyr. In his *Discourses on the First Ten
Books of Livy* (1531), Machiavelli draws the contrast between
the two conceptions of heroism:

The Pagan religion deified only men who had achieved great glory,
such as commanders of armies and chiefs of republics, whilst ours
glorifies more the humble and contemplative men than the men of
action. Our religion, moreover, places the supreme good in humility,
lowliness, and a contempt for worldly objects, while the other, on
the contrary, places the supreme good in grandeur of soul, strength
of body, and all such other qualities as render men formidable; and
if our religion claims of us fortitude of soul, it is more to enable us
to suffer than to achieve great deeds.   (285)

In Nietzsche's account of the origin of Christianity, he
views it as a conscious reaction against the ethos of the
classical world. What was regarded as good or noble by the
Greeks and Romans is damned as evil in Christianity, while
what was regarded as bad or base by the Greeks and Romans
is prized as good in Christianity. More specifically, the pride
and power of the classical hero is regarded as the height of sin

in Christian terms, while the suffering of the hero's victim is reinterpreted as the result of conscious choice and hence becomes a virtue: the Christian martyr claims to will his suffering. As Rabelais's Grangousier defines the situation of the modern European in Book I of *Gargantua and Pantagruel* (1532): 'To imitate the ancient Herculeses, Alexanders, Hannibals, Scipios, Caesars and that ilk is contrary to the profession of the Gospel . . . Is it not true that what the Saracens and Barbarians once called prowess, we term wickedness and brigandry?' (121).

Heroism in the Renaissance epic tradition

To insist upon the contrast between Achilles and Jesus may seem like labouring the obvious, but given the uncritical way in which the concept of Christian humanism has often been applied in studies of the Renaissance, it is necessary to recall how basically incompatible Christianity and classicism are, and how much redefinition and reinterpretation of central concepts such as heroism were necessary to give even the appearance of a synthesis of the two traditions. This process can be observed in the Renaissance epic. Critics in the age tended to regard the epic as the highest form of literature, rating it even higher than tragedy, and they accordingly felt that modern literature could not claim to have equalled ancient until it could offer its equivalent of the *Iliad* or the *Aeneid*. But one cannot separate the classical epic from a particular view of human nature, and especially a celebration of a particular form of aristocratic and martial virtue. Thus imitating the ancient epic presented a problem for writers in Christian Europe. They had to be mindful of Erasmus's warning in his *The Education of a Christian Prince* (1516): 'You have allied yourself with Christ – and yet will you slide back into the ways of Julius and Alexander the Great?' (153).

An epic hero like Achilles was on the whole too bloodthirsty and barbaric for Renaissance sensibilities. That is why authors in the era tended to prefer the *Aeneid* as a model, for Virgil had already to some extent civilised and domesticated the classical hero in the form of his pious Aeneas. In many respects, Virgil's Aeneas more closely resembles Homer's Hector, while Achilles appears in the *Aeneid* in the form of Turnus, the warrior Aeneas must defeat. In Virgil, the hero who serves a city and subordinates himself to its needs triumphs over the Achillean lone wolf, primarily interested in his own glory. But even the *Aeneid* clashes with Christian principles. The poem does after all celebrate the imperial ambitions and achievements of Rome, and although its hero pursues a purpose larger than personal glory, his goals are still patriotic and bound up with the pagan ideal of earthly fame.

The answer a number of Renaissance authors found to the dilemma of how to combine an epic celebration of martial heroism with Christian principles was the idea of a crusade. If a noble hero could be shown battling on behalf of Christianity against pagan enemies, then whatever ferocity he displayed would have a religious justification. He would be fighting not on behalf of his country − or at least not merely on behalf of his country − but on behalf of the one true faith and thus for the sake of eternal glory and salvation. One can see this development in Ariosto's *Orlando Furioso* (1516), and it becomes clearest in the greatest of the Italian Renaissance epics, Tasso's *Gerusalemme Liberata* (1575). A hero fighting to deliver Jerusalem from Saracen hands seems like the ideal subject for a Christian epic. In England, Spenser carried the Christianising of the epic even further. In *The Faerie Queene* (1590, 1596), Spenser's knights represent or champion some highly un-Aristotelian and unclassical virtues, such as Holiness and Chastity. It is no accident that Spenser turned for his subject matter to the Middle Ages and the legends of King Arthur and his knights. For with their conception of chivalry, medieval authors had gone further than Virgil in civilising and domesticating the epic warrior. Warriors who fight on behalf of women and who practice courtly virtues will be less ferocious than Achilles, and indeed in the chivalric epic poetry of the Middle Ages the fury of the warfare is moderated by a gallantry foreign to the spirit of the *Iliad* or even the *Aeneid*.

The notion of the chivalric knight or Christian warrior thus

gave the authors of Renaissance epics the basis for claiming
that they had found a way of going beyond the classical epic,
with a new and nobler conception of heroism. One can hear
their satisfaction in the opening of Canto One of Camoens's
The Lusiads (1572), the national epic of Portugal:

> Of the wise Greek, no more the tale unfold,
> Or the Trojan, and great voyages they made.
> Of Philip's son and Trajan, leave untold
> Triumphant fame in wars which they essayed.
> I sing the Lusian spirit bright and bold,
> That Mars and Neptune equally obeyed.
> Forget all the Muse sang in ancient days,
> For valor nobler yet is now to praise.   (I.3)

But, in his portrayal of the voyage of Vasco de Gama, has
Camoens really come up with a higher, spiritualised version
of heroism, transcending anything portrayed in the ancient
world? Or has he merely spread a veneer of spirituality over
an enterprise as worldly as anything undertaken by Achilles
or Aeneas? The fact that *The Lusiads* celebrates the colonial
ambitions of Portugal suggests that its high-mindedness may
be largely a facade. In his closing address to his King in Canto
Ten, Camoens shows that his sympathies are evenly divided
between the spiritual and the commercial:

> And hold your cavaliers in high esteem
> For, with their burning blood that knows no dread,
> Not only they exalt the Faith supreme
> But far abroad your splendid empire spread.   (X.151)

In Canto Seven, in his exhortation to European conquerors,
Camoens is even blunter:

> Such riches may perhaps your spirits spur,
> Whose hearts the Holy Temple cannot stir.   (VII.11)

I do not mean to single out Camoens as a hypocrite, but
merely to use the example of *The Lusiads* to suggest that
the fusion of classicism and Christianity in Renaissance epic
was deeply problematic, and did not always and necessarily
yield a stable synthesis. One must be alert to the possibility
that Christianity became corrupted in the process of being

incorporated into the alien form of the classical epic, that instead of raising classical heroism to a new level of spirituality, Christianity was lowered into the service of worldly ends such as colonial expansion. Certainly not everyone in the Renaissance was happy with efforts to put Christian content in classical forms, for the result in the eyes of many − including the leaders of the Reformation − was not the Christianising of paganism but the paganising of Christianity. One man who questioned the whole enterprise of the Renaissance epic was John Milton. This may sound odd, since Milton's *Paradise Lost* (1667) has been called the greatest of all Renaissance epics. And yet even as the poem provides the culmination of the form, *Paradise Lost* fundamentally overturns the Renaissance epic tradition, splitting the alliance previous authors had tried to forge between classical and Christian virtue.

Milton's plans for the long poem he felt destined to write show that he originally had in mind a more conventional Renaissance epic. Among other subjects, he considered basing an epic on the story of King Arthur, which might have resulted in a poem resembling *The Faerie Queene*. But aside from the fact that Milton simply came to doubt the historical authenticity of accounts of King Arthur, his disillusionment with English politics during the 1650s probably discouraged him from pursuing a subject that would inevitably have been patriotic in theme. By choosing instead the story of Adam and Eve, who as the progenitors of the human race cannot be pinned down to a single national origin and hence can lay claim to universal interest, Milton broke with the long-standing tradition that an epic poem should be national in character. One can see the polemical thrust of *Paradise Lost* as an epic in Milton's reflections on his choice of subject matter:

> Since first this Subject for Heroic Song
> Pleas'd me long choosing, and beginning late;
> Not sedulous by Nature to indite
> Wars, hitherto the only Argument
> Heroic deem'd, chief maistry to dissect

> With long and tedious havoc fabl'd Knights
> In Battles feign'd; the better fortitude
> Of Patience and Heroic Martyrdom
> Unsung.   (IX.25–33)

Milton explicitly contrasts the Christian notion of passive virtue with the classical notion of active, and clearly prefers the former while rejecting the celebration of warfare as a noble activity in the classical epic. He insists that he is offering an 'argument / Not less but more Heroic than the wrath / Of stern *Achilles*' (IX.13–15), thereby summing up the Christian revaluation of classical values.

The classical virtues do appear in *Paradise Lost*, but they are given to Satan and the other devils. Milton's Satan is the hypertrophy of a classical hero: he has all the pride, vengefulness, and self-reliance of Achilles, coupled with the guile, resourcefulness, and rhetorical skill of Odysseus, and like Aeneas he feels destined to found a new state. Viewing Satan in the context of the Renaissance debate between classical and Christian values helps to account for the long-standing controversy over whether he is the hero of *Paradise Lost*. In a technical sense Satan *is* the hero of *Paradise Lost* – that is, he is the one who embodies the virtues of the traditional epic hero – but Milton suggests that those virtues are demonic. The active heroism of Satan is contrasted unfavourably in the poem with the passive heroism of Christ, who is willing to sacrifice himself humbly so that God's will may be fulfilled. (This contrast is admittedly blurred in the least satisfactory part of the poem, the battle in heaven, in which Milton wants to have it both ways and insists on attributing traditional martial virtue to Christ and the good angels.) Adam and Eve are poised between the competing ethical models of Satan and Christ. As long as they passively accept their subordinate places in the order of creation, they prosper, but as soon as they heed Satan and try to become self-reliant like classical heroes, they fall.

Paradise Lost is usually considered one of the great monuments of Christian humanism, and yet the poem actually embodies a polemic against classical values. To be sure, the poem is steeped in classical learning: its texture is a rich interweaving of classical and Christian elements and to that extent represents a synthesis of the two traditions. But one cannot look simply at the *presence* of classical references; one must consider their *function*, and the fact is that they work systematically to denigrate classical values. Milton thus shows how much conflict lies hidden beneath the seemingly simple label 'Christian humanism'. No one in the Renaissance had a more comprehensive knowledge of the classical and the Christian traditions, and yet no one was more acutely aware of how antithetical they are.

Thus what is fascinating about the Renaissance is precisely the rich variety of conflicting intellectual and ethical positions it produced, resulting in part from the encounter of two traditions which were already highly developed and which challenged each other's fundamental assumptions. Wherever one turns in the Renaissance, one finds different forms of combining the classical with the Christian. Take the case of Christopher Marlowe's *Doctor Faustus* (1592). In the magician's desire to conjure up the shade of Helen of Troy, Marlowe found a perfect emblem for the inner meaning of the Renaissance. Faustus quite literally wants to revive classical antiquity within modern Europe, and through his poetry, Marlowe succeeds in making Greece come alive again on the stage. In one brilliant line – 'Instead of Troy shall Wittenberg be sacked' (V.i.105) – Marlowe manages to capture the thrust of the whole Renaissance, as Faustus hopes to see the city of Luther displace the city of Hector.

But Marlowe's portrayal of a revived antiquity is ambiguous. Helen represents the perfection of pagan beauty, but in Christian terms she is a succubus, a demon leading Faustus to his damnation; a healthy pagan appreciation of the flesh appears in a new light as the sin of lust. Marlowe maintains a dual perspective on the action: Faustus covets all the goods of the ancient world – wealth, power, beauty, wisdom – but in the Christian context of the play they have a way of turning into the Seven Deadly Sins. Perhaps Marlowe suggested the formula of *Paradise Lost* to Milton: already in *Doctor Faustus*

classical virtue appears as demonic vice. Marlowe's difference
from Milton is that his sympathies seem more evenly divided
between the classical and the Christian. He shows Faustus
damned, but also conveys a sense of his wasted nobility. And
given the sensuous power of Marlowe's verse, we come to feel
the strong attraction of the pagan goods which draw Faustus
to what in Christian terms is damnation. In *Doctor Faustus*,
we begin to see how the conflict between classical and Christian values can provide the basis of tragedy.

Tragedy and Renaissance man

Until the mention of *Doctor Faustus*, our discussion of the
Renaissance epic tradition may have seemed to be leading us
far afield from *Hamlet*. But in fact the broader the literary
context in which we view the play, the richer it will appear and
the clearer its place in world literature will become. Our
discussion of Renaissance epic has uncovered the wide spectrum of possibilities for heroism available to the age. The
variety of heroic models is reflected in the diversity of
Shakespeare's tragic heroes, who range from the pure man of
action, Coriolanus, to the introspective and contemplative
Hamlet. But even within a single play – above all in *Hamlet*
– the whole gamut of Renaissance heroic possibilities may be
present. Hamlet himself feels that he has to choose between
passive and active forms of heroism:

> Whether 'tis nobler in the mind to suffer
> The slings and arrows of outrageous fortune
> Or to take arms against a sea of troubles
> And by opposing end them. (III.i.57–60)

As we shall see, what is distinctive about Hamlet is precisely
that his mind is open to all the competing models of heroism
available in the Renaissance. He can admire martial virtue
and is haunted by thoughts of the grandeur of classical antiquity, but at the same time he is acutely aware of how Christianity has altered the terms of heroic action and called into
question traditional ideas of heroism.

Thus a survey of the Renaissance epic tradition can help us

understand the basis of Shakespearean tragedy. Renaissance epics reflect the tendency of the age to try to bring together disparate realms of value, most notably the classical and the Christian, but other values normally thought of as antithetical as well. As one can see in the knights of *The Faerie Queene*, Renaissance epic heroes often try to embody public and private virtues, to pursue both the active and the contemplative lives, to be at once fierce warriors and courteous lovers. But these attempts at arriving at a higher synthesis of antithetical values can end up highlighting the conflicts between them. For example, in Book VI of *The Faerie Queene*, Spenser's attempt to show a hero bridging the gap between the artificial world of the court and the pastoral world of nature may in fact serve to reveal just how difficult such a transition is, and thus uncover the tension between nature and convention. In a strange way, the tragic conflicts of Shakespearean tragedy grow out of the would-be harmonies of Spenserian romance (only to seek reconciliation again in Shakespeare's own romances at the end of his career).

To understand this point more fully, I wish to turn to what I regard as the most satisfactory and comprehensive theory of tragedy, the one developed in Hegel's *Aesthetics*. Hegel argues that a tragic situation involves a conflict between two goods, not a conflict between good and evil. A straightforward confrontation of good and evil is a fundamentally melodramatic situation. If good triumphs we rejoice, and if evil triumphs we lament, and in either case our sympathies are clear-cut and there is nothing in the outcome to perplex us. But in a dramatic situation in which both sides have a legitimate claim on our sympathies, no outcome can provide a simple resolution of our feelings. No matter which side wins, we feel that something good has been defeated or destroyed. In a genuinely tragic situation, we cannot see any harmless way out of the conflict, because a reconciliation of the opposing forces would require one antagonist to abandon the legitimate principle he or she stands for, and thereby sacrifice his or her integrity. That is why a tragic situation is so deeply perplexing: it calls into question our easy and unthinking assumption that the goods of this world ought to be compatible, that one should not have to choose between one's love and one's honour, for example, or between one's country and one's best friend.

For Hegel, the tragedy *par excellence* is Sophocles' *Antigone*. Insisting on leaving the traitor Polyneices unburied, Creon stands up for the good of the city. Insisting on her right to bury her brother, Antigone stands up for the good of the family. With right on both sides in such a conflict, we react to a tragedy with mixed emotions, the peculiar combination of pity and fear Aristotle thought characteristic of tragic response. (This is a hint of how the Hegelian theory of tragedy can subsume its principal rival, the Aristotelian.)

Hegel's theory of tragedy suggests why the Renaissance became such a great age of tragic drama. If tragedy involves the conflict of two goods, then it ought to flourish in an age in which competing systems of values lead to such conflicts. Hegel's theory thus suggests that the creation of tragedy is most likely to happen at the great turning points of history. When a new order is replacing the old, situations are likely to arise in which people lack clear-cut ethical guidance. With some maintaining their allegiance to the old order, others embracing the new, and still others caught in between, tragic conflicts become inevitable. The two great periods of tragic drama − fifth-century B.C. Athens and Elizabethan England − conform to this Hegelian historical schema. One of the most profound students of Hegel, the Hungarian Marxist Georg Lukács, developed this historical aspect of Hegel's theory of tragedy in his book *The Historical Novel*:

It is certainly no accident that the great periods of tragedy coincide with the great, world-historical changes in human society. Already Hegel . . . saw in the conflict of Sophocles' *Antigone* the clash of those social forces which in reality led to the destruction of primitive forms of society and to the rise of the Greek polis. Bachofen's analysis of Aeschylus' *Oresteia* . . . formulates the social conflict more concretely, i.e. as a tragic collision between the dying matriarchal order and the new patriarchal social order . . .

The position is similar with regard to the second flowering of tragedy during the Renaissance. This time the world-historical

collision between dying feudalism and the birth pangs of the final
class society [capitalism] provides the preconditions in subject-
matter and form for the resurgence of drama.   (97)

Lukács combines a brilliant theoretical insight with a degree
of dogmatism. His Marxism leads him to stress the socio-
economic conflicts in the Renaissance and to ignore the ethical
conflicts as thinkers in the age itself conceived them, which he
would no doubt dismiss as the mere ideological superstructure of
a more basic class conflict between the established feudal
aristocracy and the emerging capitalist forces in Renaissance
Europe. Lukács takes a diachronic rather than a synchronic view
of the Renaissance; that is, rather than dwelling on the conflicts
within the Renaissance as an age that tried to embrace antithetical
values, he views it as the transition *between* one set of values and
another, in short, between the medieval and the modern worlds.
This is typical of Marxist analyses of the Renaissance, in which
it tends to lose its integrity as a distinct period and dissolve into
a turning point in the march of history as Marx conceived it. Fortunately we do not have to accept the details of Lukács's interpretation of Shakespeare in order to grant the soundness of his
larger point — that the many sources of conflict within the hybrid
culture of the Renaissance provided fertile ground for the creation of tragedy.

To sum up the connection between *Hamlet* and the
Renaissance, what we think of as the optimistic programme of
the age provided in a peculiar way the formula for tragedy. The
modern use of the term 'Renaissance man', vulgarised as it may
have become, does embody an important truth about the era. It
was guided by an ideal of human totality, of trying to develop all
sides of human nature harmoniously. In the heroes of Renaissance epic as well as in historical figures from Leonardo da
Vinci to Sir Philip Sidney, we can see this ideal celebrated: to be
a painter, a scientist and an inventor all at once, or a poet, a
soldier and a courtier. As we have seen, to achieve these kinds of
syntheses, one has to bring into conjunction realms of value
normally kept apart. The hope is to reconcile them, but by bringing them into close conjunction, one may well end up being
forced to think through how really incompatible the values are.

By demanding so much of human beings, the Renaissance ideal of totality pushed human nature to its limits and thereby uncovered the great theme of tragedy: the ultimate incompatibility of different human desires and aspirations. This process is encapsulated in the opening monologue of *Doctor Faustus*, which is as full an expression of the ideal of Renaissance man as one could find, and yet one which veers in the direction of tragedy. Having surveyed and mastered the whole range of human knowledge and achievement, Faustus is struck not by the extent but by the limits of his power: the fact that as a man he cannot be a god. In his frustration, he turns to magic to make him omnipotent and is tragically destroyed as a result. Hamlet is no Faustian overreacher, and yet, as we shall see, his tragedy also arises out of a shattering of the Renaissance ideal of totality.

The place of *Hamlet* in Shakespeare's career

We can arrive at a similar understanding of *Hamlet* if we consider its place in Shakespeare's career as a dramatist. It is of course notoriously difficult to come to any firm conclusions about Shakespeare's development as a playwright. Even the exact chronological order of his plays is a matter of conjecture, and although patient scholarship has determined many of the facts concerning the external details of his career, we have almost no evidence on which to base any judgements about what was going on in his mind at any given point. Since his works are our only real window into Shakespeare's inner life, attempts to explain them in biographical terms easily degenerate into circular reasoning. Not wanting to get involved in this sort of speculation, I will confine myself to the most general observations on what I see as the relation of *Hamlet* to Shakespeare's earlier plays.

Hamlet was written probably sometime in 1600 or 1601, that is, at the beginning of the period of Shakespeare's mature tragedies. In order of composition, it probably falls between *Julius Caesar* (1599) and *Othello* (1604). The first half of Shakespeare's career was devoted largely to comedies and histories, though it included two tragedies, *Titus Andronicus* (1594) and *Romeo and Juliet* (1595). The most

sustained achievement of the first half of Shakespeare's
career is the so-called Second Tetralogy of history plays:
Richard II (1595), *Henry IV, Parts One and Two* (1596, 1598),
and *Henry V* (1599). Though these plays move back and forth
between the poles of tragedy and comedy, in many respects
their impulse is epic, so much so that some critics have been led
to dub them *The Henriad. Henry V* even begins with an invoca-
tion to the Muse, and in general these plays build up to a
celebration of one of England's great military victories, Henry
V's triumph over the French at Agincourt. If an epic is a work
which helps shape a people's sense of their national identity by
giving them a portrait of their historical origins as well as of their
distinctive virtues embodied in one of their great martial heroes,
then the Second Tetralogy can lay claim to being the authentic
English epic.

What is of particular interest to us is that together the Henry
plays constitute a portrait of a Renaissance man. I do not wish
to make Shakespeare sound programmatic, but he does show the
figure of Prince Hal/Henry V spanning all the normally warring
opposites of Renaissance life. Henry is a Protean figure: he can
move back and forth between the tavern and the battlefield, talk
to commoners as well as nobles, lead in both wartime and
peacetime, succeed both as a lover and as a warrior, switch from
sorrowful compassion to angry rage at a moment's notice. By
placing Henry initially between the two poles of Falstaff and
Hotspur, Shakespeare shows him learning from both models and
ultimately synthesising a more comprehensive excellence out of
the antithetical virtues embodied in the pleasure-loving Falstaff
and the spirited Hotspur. By the time Henry comes to the throne,
even initial skeptics like the Archbishop of Canterbury speak of
him in glowing terms as a Renaissance man, adept in all areas of
human endeavour:

> Hear him but reason in divinity,
> And all-admiring, with an inward wish
> You would desire the King were made a prelate;
> Hear him debate of commonwealth affairs,
> You would say it hath been all his study;
> List his discourse of war, and you shall hear
> A fearful battle rend'red you in music.   (I.i.38–44)

Canterbury even sees Henry as a kind of philosopher-king, uniting the active and contemplative lives:

> So that the art and practic part of life
> Must be the mistress to this theoric.   (I.i.51–2)

One aspect of Henry's comprehensiveness is his ability to encompass both classical and Christian virtues, reflected in Shakespeare's imagery when he pictures Henry's army 'Following the mirror of all Christian Kings, / With winged heels, as English Mercuries' (II.Chorus. 6–7). Henry has all the martial virtues of the classical epic hero, but at the appropriate moments he tempers them with a Christian humility and mercy. The only time Henry feels awkward making the transition from one area of life to another occurs when he must leave the battlefield and learn how to woo the French princess Katherine for his wife. But even here, Henry succeeds in turning his seeming lack of courtly eloquence to his advantage and wins the day. By ending the play with Henry's proposed marriage, Shakespeare gives a comic shape to his career and indeed to the whole Second Tetralogy. Despite the many tragic moments in the plays, Henry's own story is comic in outcome because of his ability to synthesise a larger whole out of the antithetical values of his world.

But Henry V is a rare figure in Shakespeare, perhaps the only ruler to enjoy this kind of comprehensive success. And Shakespeare reminds us in the closing chorus of *Henry V* that the kingdom fell apart after Henry's death, because of the weakness of his son as ruler. Even within the plays, we get a sense of the fragility of his achievement; we can feel the tension as he tries to reconcile the opposing forces in his world. That is how the comic resolutions of *Henry V* set the stage for the great tragic period of Shakespeare's career. It is as if Shakespeare made one last attempt in *Henry V* to hold together the Renaissance synthesis, to create a hero on the model of the chivalric knights and crusaders of Renaissance epic. But in the process, he appears to have become more fully aware of the problematic character of such syntheses of

antithetical values. I realise the dangers of artificially imposing a pattern on Shakespeare's career, and therefore I put
foward this view of the relation of *Henry V* to the tragedies
tentatively and as a working hypothesis. It is at least worth
reflecting on the fact that Shakespeare attempted a portrait of
a kind of Renaissance man in the last play he wrote before
embarking upon his great series of tragedies (most scholars
believe that *Julius Caesar* followed *Henry V* in Shakespeare's
career).

The antithetical values which Henry V manages to hold
together are exactly what tear Shakespeare's later tragic
heroes apart. For example, Henry V is able to make a smooth
transition from wartime to peacetime as a ruler, recognising
that he must act humbly with his people even though his
military victories give him much of which to be proud. This
is precisely the transition Coriolanus cannot make: he brings
on his tragedy by his failure to distinguish between how one
treats a foreign enemy and how one treats a fellow citizen.
The dilemma of the warrior trying to adapt to the demands
of civil society is one of the fundamental tragic situations in
Shakespeare. He explores the theme as early as the opening
monologue of *Richard III* (1592), and it in part provides the
basis for the tragedies of Othello and Macbeth. These
characters find that the very qualities which make them
heroes on the battlefield work against them once 'the battle's
lost and won', and they must try to fit into the settled order
of a community at peace. Othello's wooing of Desdemona is
the tragic mirror image of Henry's wooing of Katherine. Like
Henry with the French princess, Othello seems to overcome
everything that makes him alien to Desdemona's way of life
and gets her to break with the custom of her people in order
to seek a higher form of love. But in his attempt to add the
role of lover to that of warrior and thus to become a more
complete human being, Othello ends up out of his depth and
is destroyed by the machinations of Iago, who is able to prey
upon Othello's straightforwardness as a soldier to deceive
him about Desdemona. In short, the scene which provides the

comic conclusion to *Henry V* — a gruff soldier wooing a foreign beauty — provides the basis of the tragedy in *Othello*.

It was, then, in the writing of his history plays that Shakespeare discovered the subject matter for his mature tragedies. From the very beginning, the history plays portray the clashing of antithetical values, above all the tension between public and private life. As early as the *Henry VI* plays (1589–90), which are among Shakespeare's first works, he shows an awareness of the antithetical character of classical and Christian values. For example, the usurper York consciously contrasts Henry VI's passive Christian virtue with his own active classical virtue:

> That head of thine doth not become a crown:
> Thy hand is made to grasp a palmer's staff
> And not to grace an aweful princely sceptre.
> That gold must round engirt these brows of mine,
> Whose smile and frown, like to Achilles' spear,
> Is able with the change to kill and cure.
>
> (Part II, V.i.96–101)

As in Renaissance epics, Christ and Achilles are the two poles of virtue in Shakespeare's first history plays.

Thus looking at *Hamlet* in the context of Shakespeare's career confirms what we saw by looking at *Hamlet* in the broader context of the Renaissance. We can learn a great deal about *Hamlet* by studying the Renaissance, but we should also be alert to the possibility that we can learn about the Renaissance by studying *Hamlet*. Indeed no single work can offer a wider view of the era in all its many aspects — from its politics to its theatre, from its religious speculations to its sense of the past. The universality of the play is ultimately grounded in the fullness of its portrayal of its own age. *Hamlet* transcends its historical moment, not by ignoring it or leaving it behind, but by so completely capturing its essence that it becomes a prime source for later ages to understand the Renaissance. In short, the richness of *Hamlet* is in many respects the richness of the Renaissance itself. If the play strikes us as complex, a principal reason is that the age it is portraying is complex as well. I am going to argue, then, that

Hamlet is the quintessential Renaissance play, not because it is the typical Renaissance play, but because it gives us access to the heart of the Renaissance, the heart of its conflicts and contradictions, the heart of its drama. As we shall see, where the would-be Renaissance synthesis breaks down, the tragedy of *Hamlet* begins.

Chapter 2

The tragedy of Hamlet

The problem of Hamlet

The question which has preoccupied critics of *Hamlet* is: why does the prince delay in taking his revenge on the man who murdered his father? As soon as he learns of the guilt of his uncle, Claudius, he promises to 'sweep' to his 'revenge' 'with wings as swift / As meditation' (I.v.29–31). And yet he does not kill the king immediately, and his delay costs the lives of his mother, Gertrude, his beloved, Ophelia, her father, Polonius, her brother, Laertes, as well as Hamlet's old friends, Rosencrantz and Guildenstern. Frustrated by the often bizarre theories offered to explain the prince's delay, some critics have rejected the idea that any mystery surrounds his hesitation. They argue that his difficulties are external and point to the many impediments which stand in the way of his swiftly and easily killing Claudius, such as the guards who normally surround the king and Hamlet's need to produce a publicly acceptable justification for his revenge before acting.

But Shakespeare seems to have gone out of his way to indicate that Hamlet's difficulties are not merely those of outward circumstance. The episode of Laertes leading a rebellion against Claudius to avenge the death of his father, Polonius, seems designed to suggest how much more easily Hamlet could have challenged the king, especially given the fact that, as Claudius himself admits, the prince is 'lov'd of the distracted multitude' (IV.iii.4). Above all, it is Hamlet himself who raises the question of why he delays his revenge:

> I do not know
> Why yet I live to say, 'This thing's to do,'
> Sith I have cause, and will, and strength, and means
> To do't.   (IV.iv.43–6)

22

With all his searching for reasons, Hamlet never points to any external factors to explain why he fails to act. Thus the critics who look within Hamlet for reasons for his hesitation are not falsely imposing their own questions on the play but simply following the hero's lead.

One prominent approach to explaining Hamlet's delay is the psychoanalytic. First suggested by Freud himself in a footnote to *The Interpretation of Dreams* (1900), this approach was developed by Freud's biographer and disciple, Ernest Jones, in a brief book called *Hamlet and Oedipus* (1949). Reduced to its essentials, the psychoanalytic argument claims that the Oedipus complex accounts for Hamlet's failure to act. The prince hesitates to kill Claudius because he identifies too closely with his uncle as a man who has acted out Hamlet's secret desire, namely, to kill his father and marry his mother. Jones was able to point to a considerable body of evidence within the play to support his claims. Hamlet's feelings towards his mother are certainly an important element in the play, in many respects more important than his feelings towards his father. And in his intensely dramatic encounter with his mother in III.iv, Hamlet does appear to lose emotional control and to dwell upon the sexual details of his mother's relation with his uncle with an obsessiveness that borders on the pathological.

One of the attractions of the Freudian view of *Hamlet* is that it seems to account for the universal appeal of the play. If one accept Freud's claim for the universality of the Oedipus complex, the Freudian Hamlet becomes representative of humanity in his mixed feelings towards his parents. According to this argument, *Hamlet* touches us so deeply because it touches us in the deepest stratum of the unconscious. But the problem with this argument is the problem which arises in most psychoanalytic discussions of literature, especially of tragedy. In its eagerness to find the universal, psychoanalytic criticism tends to lose sight of what is distinctive in a literary character, particularly in a tragic hero. We are told that we are interested in a hero precisely because of what he has in common with us (Hamlet himself baulks when Gertrude and

Claudius try to assimilate his experience to what is common to humanity, I.ii.72–4, 89–106). And that common element usually turns out to be some form of weakness. In Jones's argument, the fundamental fact in *Hamlet* is the hero's inability to cope with the ambivalence of his feelings towards his parents, indeed his incapacity to face up to the nature of his emotions. Jones writes of Hamlet's delay: 'This paralysis arises . . . not from physical or moral cowardice, but from that intellectual cowardice, that reluctance to dare the exploration of his inmost soul, which Hamlet shares with the rest of the human race' (103). In short, for Jones what makes Hamlet a hero is his cowardice. Most psychoanalytic readings are not as reductive as this, but Jones's argument nevertheless reveals their general tendency. Freudian theory can explain the hero's behaviour only at the price of denying his authentic heroism.

Pre-Freudian analyses of Hamlet's character, however quaint and old-fashioned they may now seem, at least had the virtue of pointing to something unusual and admirable in the hero to explain the delay in his revenge. Goethe's famous theory, developed in his *Wilhelm Meister's Apprenticeship* (1795–6), presents Hamlet as a poetic and morally sensitive soul, crushed by the weight of the barbarous task of murder assigned to him. The equally famous Schlegel–Coleridge thesis views *Hamlet* as a tragedy of thought, the story of a man whose tendency to reflect profoundly on all sides of an issue prevents him from coming to any decision and hence from acting. A. C. Bradley, whose work represents the culmination of the nineteenth-century preoccupation with character analysis of Shakespeare's plays, developed a more comprehensive theory of *Hamlet*,which is still one of the most insightful discussions of the play. Bradley starts from the fact that several of Hamlet's actions, such as his murder of Polonius and his dispatching of Rosencrantz and Guildenstern to their deaths, belie the common image of him as constitutionally weak and irresolute. Bradley wishes to avoid describing a Hamlet who would never under any circumstances have been capable of dealing effectively with Claudius. For Bradley, Hamlet's tragedy stems from the fact that he has to deal with Claudius at just that moment in his life when he is incapable of doing so. Bradley offers the prince's melancholy as the explanation for the delay in his revenge, a melancholy occasioned by his father's death and above all by his mother's hasty remarriage. Her lack of loyalty to his father's memory causes Hamlet to lose faith in her, and, because of the generalising tendency of his mind, this leads him to lose faith in womankind as a whole, and, more generally still, in the power of any value to resist the ravages of time. Thus, according to Bradley, just when hamlet needs all the will he can muster to pursue his task of vengeance, his will is sapped by the collapse of his once idealistic faith in man's capabilities into a generalised despair in the efficacy of any action.

These nineteenth-century readings of *Hamlet* have greatly enriched our understanding of the play and they also preserve our sense of something extraordinary in the hero. And yet these readings still do not present a particularly *heroic* Hamlet. William Hazlitt stated explicitly what many nineteenth-century critics only implied when he wrote: 'Hamlet is as little of the hero as a man can well be' (82). Even Bradley confines himself to the idea that Hamlet can act heroically only at times and might have been more fully heroic only under different circumstances. The weakness of the nineteenth-century preoccupation with character analysis is that it leads these critics to interpret Hamlet's tragedy as essentially subjective. They all search for some element in Hamlet which makes him view his task as problematic; they do not look for anything objective in Hamlet's situation which makes his task genuinely problematic.

I am not talking about external factors which make Hamlet's task difficult to accomplish, but internal factors which might make him legitimately hesitate to pursue a single-minded course of vengeance. Many critics talk about the ghost's command to avenge his murder as if it were unconditional. But unlike other apparitions in Renaissance drama, who demand a simple and straightforward revenge, the ghost in *Hamlet* hedges in his charge with careful instructions:

> But howsomever thou pursues this act,
> Taint not thy mind, nor let thy soul contrive
> Against thy mother aught. Leave her to heaven.   (I.v.84–6)

In these lines, we can begin to see the germ of a tragic situation. Can Hamlet fulfill all the conditions of the ghost's charge or is the ghost in fact making mutually exclusive demands upon him? Above all, is there any way for Hamlet to accomplish his revenge and avoid tainting his mind? If not, then from the very beginning, the ghost places the prince in a double bind, a situation in which, no matter what he does, he will be forced to violate some legitimate principle. Analysing the play in Hegelian terms as involving a conflict of two goods has the advantage of allowing us to preserve a heroic image of Hamlet. Ernest Jones argues that what distinguishes Hamlet is his inability to see into the reality of his situation, but perhaps what is heroic about him is precisely his awareness of just how complex his dilemma is.

Even a brief review of critical approaches to *Hamlet* suggests that the challenge to any interpretation is to find a way of explaining the delay in Hamlet's vengeance without undermining our sense of him as a heroic figure. Reading most interpretations, one may feel one has come to understand Hamlet, perhaps one is ready to excuse his delay, certainly one can sympathise with his failure to act. But after such analyses is there anything left to admire in his character? We must be wary of critical approaches which are in effect patronising to Hamlet, and which cut him down to manageable size by suggesting that all his problems stem from simple ignorance, elementary errors of judgement, emotional maladjustment, or psychopathology.

It is best, then, to begin one's analysis of *Hamlet* with a recognition of the extraordinary dramatic challenge Shakespeare set himself in creating the play. Normally a hero manifests his nature in action, for example, the swift, decisive deeds of Achilles. But Hamlet's chief characteristic throughout most of the play is his hesitation to act, which makes him appear unheroic in any conventional sense. The presence in the play of more conventionally heroic types such as Laertes and the Norwegian prince, Fortinbras, only serves to emphasise the oddity of Hamlet as a hero. But if he is problematic as a hero, the reason is that heroism itself has become deeply problematic in his world (though one hastens to add that because heroism has become problematic does not mean that it has disappeared). Here is where the Renaissance background we have discussed becomes crucial to understanding the play. Hamlet's difficulties are not *merely* personal, but reflect the fundamental issues of the era in which his story is set. In particular, his personal question of action versus inaction is profoundly related to the issue of active versus passive heroism we have seen as basic to the Renaissance. Hamlet's personal story is of course fascinating in itself, but it gains its larger resonance and significance from the fact that it is rooted in a substantive ethical conflict characteristic of an entire age.

Hamlet and the revenge play tradition

If, as we have seen, the Renaissance was characterised by an uneasy alliance of classical and Christian elements, then no single issue was more perfectly calculated to expose the inner tensions of the age than revenge. Achilles and Jesus have diametrically opposed attitudes towards vengeance, and it is hard to see how anyone could reconcile the two positions. It is no accident, then, that revenge emerged as one of the central issues in Renaissanic drama, and particularly in England the so-called revenge tragedy became one of the dominant genres on the stage. To be sure, revenge is an inherently and perennially dramatic subject, and the Renaissance theatre had no monopoly on the theme, as a glance back to ancient Greek drama or forward to the latest Hollywood urban vigilante films will show. Still, given the hybrid nature of Renaissance culture, dramatists in the era were able to explore the issue of revenge with particular awareness of the range of ethical responses it can evoke.

In selecting the subject of *Hamlet*, Shakespeare chose to work within this revenge play tradition. In fact, he was not even the first to write a play called *Hamlet*. All scholars are agreed that an earlier Elizabethan play on the subject once existed, conventionally referred to as the *Ur-Hamlet*, and almost certainly written by Thomas Kyd (1558–94). All efforts to reconstruct this play, or even to arrive at any conception of its content, have been based on weak, highly speculative foundations and have ultimately proved fruitless. Fortunately we do have another revenge play by Kyd, *The Spanish Tragedy* (c. 1585–90), which was by all evidence one of the most popular plays of the English Renaissance, and most probably the one which established the revenge play genre. *The Spanish Tragedy* has much in common with Shakespeare's *Hamlet*, including a ghost calling for revenge and a play-within-the-play, together with a sustained exploration of the themes of madness and suicide.

But what makes *The Spanish Tragedy* particularly relevant to *Hamlet* is that Kyd portrays his avenger, Hieronimo, as torn between the classical and Christian attitudes towards revenge. In a long soliloquy pondering his task as an avenger, Hieronimo begins with the biblical injunction against taking revenge, and seems to be leaning towards a passive attitude of letting events take their course without his interference:

> *Vindicta mihi*!
> Ay, heaven will be revenged of every ill,
> Nor will they suffer murder unrepaid:
> Then stay, Hieronimo, attend their will,
> For mortal men may not appoint their time.   (III.xiii.1–5)

Hieronimo's first words even quote the New Testament in Latin; the full passage is: 'Dearly beloved, avenge not yourselves, but rather give place unto wrath: for it is written, Vengeance is mine; I will repay, saith the Lord' (Romans, xii.19; Authorised Version). This is the *locus classicus* for the Christian attitude towards revenge, which reserves the right of vengeance to God and forbids it to any true believer.

But Hieronimo immediately rejects the passivity of the Christian attitude, and tries to rouse himself to an active course of revenge:

Strike, and strike home, where wrong is offered thee;
For evils unto ills conductors be,
And death's the worst of resolution.
For he that thinks with patience to contend
To quiet life, his life shall easily end.   (III.xiii.7–11)

Hieronimo is directly prompted into these thoughts by his
quotation from Seneca's *Agamemnon* in the preceding line:
'Per scelus semper tutum est sceleribus iter' ('The safe path
for crime is always through crime'). Hieronimo even appears
to be carrying a copy of Seneca in this scene and goes on to
quote two lines in Latin from his *Troades*. In short, Kyd goes
out of his way to associate thoughts of active vengeance with
classical literature in Hieronimo's mind. And this is not an
isolated incident: from the very beginning Kyd identifies the
cause of revenge with the classical world. The ghost who
haunts the play and the figure of Revenge who accompanies
him rise up in the first scene out of a distinctly classical
underworld, complete with Charon, Cerberus, Minos, Aecus
and Radamanth, and even Hector and Achilles's Myrmidons
(I.i.20–49). Thus, at the fountainhead of the English revenge
play tradition, the issue of the active pursuit of revenge versus
the passive renunciation of revenge is articulated in terms of
the classical versus the Christian traditions.

Throughout its history, the revenge play proved to be an
effective vehicle for dramatising the issue of the nature of
heroism: whether the true hero is the man who gives vent to
his passions in an act of vengeance or the man who learns to
restrain his passions and forswear revenge. This contrast is
summed up neatly in Philip Massinger's *The Roman Actor*
(1626):

                              And since we cannot
        With safety use the active, let's make use of
        The passive fortitude.   (I.i.116–18)

To be sure, these ethical alternatives were not always for-
mulated in terms of a contrast between classical and Christian
attitudes. For example it was easy to find classical authorities
opposed to revenge. Take the case of John Marston's *Antonio's*

Revenge (1600–1), a strange play which resembles *Hamlet* in many details of plot. (Opinion on the exact relation of the two works varies, but current scholarship suggests that it was Marston who imitated Shakespeare.) Forswearing the conventional role of the avenger, a character named Pandulpho defends himself to his nephew in terms derived from Roman Stoicism, the school of classical philosophy that advocated self-control, showing indifference to pleasure or pain, and enduring evil calmly:

> Listen, young blood, 'tis not true valor's pride
> To swagger, quarrel, swear, stomp, rave, and chide,
> To stab in fume of blood, to keep loud coil,
> To bandy factions in domestic broils,
> To dare the act of sins whose filth excels
> The blackest customs of blind infidels.
> No, my lov'd youth, he may of valor vaunt
> Whom fortune's loudest thunder cannot daunt,
> Whom fretful galls of chance, stern fortune's siege
> Makes not his reason slink, the soul's fair liege,
> Whose well-peis'd action ever rests upon
> Not giddy honors, but discretion.
> This heart in valor even Jove out-goes.   (I.ii.323–35)

In this defence of passive over active heroism, Christian sentiments work together with classical philosophy in the form of Stoic precepts.

Still, only because Marston draws upon ancient *philosophy* do we find the classical allied with the Christian against revenge in his play. The classical *heroic* tradition, especially as embodied in the classical epics, viewed revenge as a noble activity, in some ways as *the* noble activity *par excellence*. Renaissance revenge plays continued this association of revenge with an aristocratic *ethos*. The fact that duelling was regarded as an aristocratic privilege in the Renaissance is a practical reflection of how the issue of disregarding public forms of justice and taking the law into one's own hands was linked to notions of aristocratic virtue. The identification of the spirit of honour with the spirit of revenge was even closer in the Spanish plays of the Renaissance than in the English. In Lope de Vega's *Peribáñez* (*c*.1610), for example, a peasant kills his lord in revenge for attacking his wife, but instead of being punished for the deed, he is rewarded. The King of Castile is so struck by a peasant displaying such an aristocratic concern for his honour that he makes him a captain in his army and grants him the right to bear arms as a gentleman.

In English Renaissance theatre, *The Atheist's Tragedy* (1611) by Cyril Tourneur formulates the issue of revenge explicitly in terms of the contrast between aristocratic and Christian virtue. The hero-villain of the play, D'Amville (the atheist of the title), is a spokesman for the aristocratic notion of active virtue, especially as manifested in martial virtue:

> O noble war! Thou first original
> Of all man's honour. How dejectedly
> The baser spirit of our present time
> Hath cast itself below the ancient worth
> Of our forefathers, from whose noble deeds
> Ignobly we derive our pedigrees!   (I.i.67–72)

Juxtaposed with D'Amville is the young hero Charlemont. After D'Amville kills Charlemont's father, Montferrers, we would expect the young man to seek revenge. But in a reversal of dramatic expectations, the ghost of Montferrers appears to Charlemont to counsel him *against* revenge:

> Attend with patience the success of things.
> But leave revenge unto the king of kings.   (II.vi.21–2)

The counterpoising of Christian patience against his instincts to avenge his father places Charlemont in a tragic dilemma, made clear when in an inversion of *Hamlet* the ghost reappears to Charlemont to blunt his almost whetted purpose:

> *Montferrers* Hold, Charlemont!
> Let him revenge my murder and thy wrongs
> To whom the justice of revenge belongs.
> *Charlemont*   You torture me between the passion of my blood and
> the religion of my soul.   (III.ii.35–9)

Torn between his sense of honour and his Christian beliefs, Charlemont provides an emblem of the dilemma of the Renaissance revenger. What is unusual about Charlemont is that he eventually triumphs over D'Amville precisely by a form of passive resistance:

> Only to Heaven I attribute the work,
> Whose gracious motives made me still forbear
> To be mine own revenger. Now I see
> That patience is the honest man's revenge.   (V.ii.268–71)

This redefinition of *revenge* – inaction viewed as the most effective form of action – is a Christian revaluation of values in the exact Nietzschean sense.

But Hamlet cannot find such an easy way to resolve his dilemma. As one reads the wide range of English Renaissance revenge plays, one senses that they are dealing with the same issues as *Hamlet*, but not dealing with them as profoundly. Hieronimo momentarily wavers between forswearing and pursuing his revenge, but quickly resolves to take the active course, and does so implacably. Charlemont is similarly divided between action and inaction, and though he chooses the course opposite to Hieronimo's, he sticks to his resolve with the same determination. By comparison with Hamlet, characters like Hieronimo and Charlemont inevitably appear one-dimensional. What Shakespeare did was to cast an unusually thoughtful man in the role of the revenger, and thus allowed Hamlet to reveal the many facets of the issue of revenge.

Hamlet and classical heroism

Even our brief survey of the revenge play tradition and the way it dramatised the ethical conflicts of the Renaissance gives some sense of the forces which are polarised in Hamlet's soul. On one side are all the impulses which impel him towards revenge, the heroic ethos which demands that he repay violence with violence, an ethos associated in the play with the world of classical antiquity but also with the pagan past of Denmark. On the other side are all the factors which make him hesitate to take revenge, the factors which complicate his task by opening up a perspective on revenge unknown to the ancient or the pagan worlds. These forces are bound up in complex ways with Hamlet's Christianity, and above all with the fact that his horizons are not limited to this world. In some ways, the figure of the ghost encapsulates the polarities Hamlet faces. As the ghost of his *father*, dressed in military garb and crying for revenge, it conjures up the world of epic warfare and heroic combat. But as the *ghost* of his father, rising out of what appears to be purgatory, it shatters the narrow bounds of the pagan imagination and opens a window on the eternal vistas of Christianity. In short, the ghost is at one and the same time a pagan and a Christian figure, and as such points to the heart of Hamlet's tragic dilemma as a modern Christian charged with the ancient pagan task of revenge.

The opening of *Hamlet* is dominated by this ominous, mysterious, and profoundly ambiguous figure of the ghost. It stalks across the stage as a powerful reminder of the possibilities of the heroic life:

> Such was the very armor he had on
> When he the ambitious Norway combated.
> So frown'd he once when in an angry parle
> He smote the sledded Polacks on the ice.   (I.i.60–3)

We learn that the elder Hamlet triumphed over Fortinbras of Norway in single combat, thereby winning territory for his country and glory for himself. This contest of hero against hero – 'prick'd on by a most emulate pride' (I.i.83) – calls up images of the world of Norse saga, from which the story of Hamlet is in fact ultimately derived. The earliest written version of the legend dates from the second half of the twelfth century, recorded in the *Historiae Danicae* of Saxo Grammaticus (the story may have reached Shakespeare via a French reworking of Saxo, by François de Belleforest, published in 1576 in his *Histoires Tragiques*). In its original version, the Hamlet story is considerably more primitive than Shakespeare's, incorporating all the brutal and barbaric elements typical of the blood feuds portrayed in Norse saga. For example, in Saxo the Hamlet figure finally sets fire to his uncle's palace, burning all its occupants while they sleep. For all that Shakespeare did to modernise the story, something of this pagan aura survives in his version, in particular surrounding the elder Hamlet.

Although there is obviously something frightening about the ghost, there is something 'majestical' (I.i.143) about it as well. With its 'martial stalk' (I.i.66) and 'fair and warlike form' (I.i.47), it symbolises the heroic past of Denmark, an age when men settled their differences openly and courageously by hand-to-hand combat, following explicit and well-defined rules (I.i.86–95). The story of the struggle between the elder Hamlet and the elder Fortinbras provides a context in which to view the events which occur in the play, a standard of heroic conduct by which to measure the sordidness and shabbiness of the intrigue, infighting and backstabbing which characterise the court of Claudius. The elder Hamlet is only a few weeks dead, and yet a gulf already seems to separate his world from that of the play. The elevated, epic diction with which characters describe his ghost has a distancing effect, conveying a sense of him as a figure out of the remote rather than the recent past. The appearance of the ghost makes Hamlet's friend, Horatio, think of ancient Roman history, of the omens which heralded the death of Julius Caesar (I.i.113–16).

Thus memories of the heroic past of Denmark begin to fuse in *Hamlet* with broader memories of the classical heroic tradition. As Reuben Brower has shown in his book *Hero and Saint*, the language applied to the ghost is derived from the Elizabethan heroic idiom, developed in the process of translating Homer and Virgil into English. Brower points specifically to formulaic epithets like 'the ambitious Norway' and 'the sledded Polacks' as Homeric characteristics of the style of the speeches which describe the ghost. Hamlet himself, as a good Renaissance scholar, explicitly and repeatedly associates his father with the classical world:

> See what a grace was seated on this brow:
> Hyperion's curls, the front of Jove himself,
> An eye like Mars, to threaten and command,
> A station like the herald Mercury.   (III.iv.55–8)

> So excellent a king, that was to this
> Hyperion to a satyr . . .
> My father's brother, but no more like my father
> Than I to Hercules.   (I.ii.139–40, 152–3)

Similarly, when Hamlet feels the need to summon up an image
of heroic resolve, he asks one of the actors who has come to
the Danish court for a speech about the slaughter of Priam,
a speech which in both style and subject matter calls to mind
Homer and Virgil, and above all the *Iliad*. Appropriately in
a scene depicting Achilles's son avenging his father's death,
Pyrrhus presents a powerful image of the hypertrophy of the
classical revenge ethic:

> A roused vengeance sets him new a-work,
> And never did the Cyclops' hammers fall
> On Mars's armor, forg'd for proof eterne
> With less remorse than Pyrrhus' bleeding sword
> Now falls on Priam.   (II.ii.488–92)

It is important to realise that, as bookish as Hamlet may
seem at times to be, the classical world is not a literary
abstraction for him. He has a genuine sense of what it is to
be heroic in the classical mould. The various theories about
his mild or reflective nature have tended to obscure the hard
edge in Shakespeare's portrait. This aspect comes out, for
example, in the prince's interest in fencing, a dramatic detail
which is obviously required for Shakespeare's ending, but
which also does a great deal to develop our sense of Hamlet
as a heroic type. When trying to entrap him, Claudius knows
that he can rely on his rivalry with Laertes, since the prince
has obviously become jealous of his fellow countryman's
reputation as a swordsman (IV.vii.102–5). As his final confrontation with Laertes approaches, Hamlet gives an astute
analysis of his situation in the face of Horatio's friendly
doubts:

Horatio   You will lose this wager, my lord.
Hamlet   I do not think so; since he went into France I have been
            in continual practice. I shall win at the odds.
                                              (V.ii.209–11)

This is a revealing detail: with all that is on his mind, Hamlet has somehow found time in between soliloquies to work on his parries and his *flèche* attacks. He evidently cannot stand the thought that another young man at court should be regarded as a better fencer than he. Moreover, he has the good athlete's sense of precisely where he stands *vis-à-vis* the competition. He does not idly boast to Horatio of annihilating an inferior opponent, but carefully calculates that his handicap is just enough to give him the victory.

The final duelling scene of *Hamlet* balances the first, as the original talk of the elder Hamlet's combat with the elder Fortinbras finds its distant and diminished echo in the fencing match of the younger Hamlet and Laertes. The forthrightness and fair play of the first contest only serve to highlight the duplicity involved in the second, a contest rigged on so many levels that a just outcome becomes impossible. Indeed, considering the first and last scenes of *Hamlet* together gives some sense of the historical distance travelled in the course of the play. The original Hamlet–Fortinbras combat begins to appear at least faintly archaic, if not anachronistic in the Denmark we have come to know in the intervening acts. There is something medieval or feudal about the Hamlet–Fortinbras encounter, almost as if it were a chivalric trial by combat.

The concluding Hamlet–Laertes duel, by contrast, strikes us as fully modern, with plots, counterplots and counter-counterplots, and layers of meaning concealing still deeper layers of meaning. A fencing match with poisoned rapiers, in which Laertes serves as proxy for Claudius in the king's struggle with Hamlet and a poisoned drink stands ready to finish off the prince, is clearly a more subtle and sophisticated event than the simple confrontation between the elder Hamlet and the elder Fortinbras. The duel conjures up images of Machiavelli and scheming Renaissance princes like the Borgias rather than of Homer and Achilles. Thus what makes the Hamlet–Laertes combat seem more modern is precisely what makes it also seem less noble and less heroic. Unlike the elder Hamlet and the elder Fortinbras, Hamlet and Laertes are not openly fighting on behalf of their nations, and, though their combat turns out to be mortal, it was supposed to be mere sport. Only treachery produces the fatal results and gives the duel a larger, political significance.

Still, the fact that the would-be heroic impulses of Hamlet and Laertes are channelled into such devious and indirect paths does not mean that heroism has become wholly a thing of the past in their world. What we must trace in *Hamlet* is precisely the complication and distortion of ancient heroism as it is transposed into a distinctly modern setting. However different the terms and outcome, Hamlet and Laertes are 'prick'd on' to their combat by the same 'emulate pride' which motivated the elder Hamlet and the elder Fortinbras. One reason Shakespeare paired Laertes with Hamlet is to bring out the prince's spiritedness by giving him someone with whom to compare himself. Once Laertes finds himself in the same situation as Hamlet − called upon to avenge the murder of his father, Polonius − this comparison becomes unavoidable, as the prince himself notes (V.ii.77–8). In particular, Laertes functions as a model of the absoluteness of the revenge ethic, the way it seeks to reject all competing values and loyalties:

> To hell, allegiance! vows, to the blackest devil!
> Conscience and grace, to the profoundest pit!
> I dare damnation. To this point I stand,
> That both the worlds I give to negligence,
> Let come what comes, only I'll be reveng'd
> Most thoroughly for my father. (IV.v.132–7)

In a pointed exchange with Claudius, Laertes vehemently expresses the Renaissance avenger's conflict between what Tourneur's Charlemont called the passion of his blood and the religion of his soul:

King   What would you undertake
      To show yourself in deed your father's son
      More than in words?
Laertes   To cut his throat i' th' church.
King No place indeed should murder sanctuarize,
      Revenge should have no bounds. (IV.vii.124–8)

In the very act of rejecting them, Laertes reveals the forces which stand opposed to the swift and singleminded accomplishment of revenge in the world of *Hamlet*. Hamlet would have to be a much simpler character than he is to thrust aside all religious scruples about the morality of revenge, as Laertes claims to do (and even he has a fit of conscience in the final scene, V.ii.296).

Indeed Hamlet is more complex than Laertes and thus does not rush into the first opportunity for revenge that presents itself to him. Nevertheless, though Hamlet's soul embraces many elements that are lacking in Laertes's, he does share the element of spiritedness with his companion. Laertes seems to be the character most capable of bringing out Hamlet's competitiveness, perhaps because they are fellow citizens and grew up together. Their rivalry reaches a fever pitch when they confront each other at Ophelia's grave, and Hamlet feels compelled to prove that he loved her more than her brother did:

> 'Swounds, show me what thou't do.
> Woo't weep, woo't fight, woo't fast, woo't tear thyself?
> Woo't drink up eisel, eat a crocodile?
> I'll do't. Dos't thou come here to whine?
> To outface me with leaping in her grave?
> Be buried quick with her, and so will I.
> And if thou prate of mountains, let them throw
> Millions of acres on us, till our ground,
> Singeing his pate against the burning zone,
> Make Ossa like a wart! Nay, and thou'lt mouth,
> I'll rant as well as thou.   (V.i.274–84)

There is something of the almost childish contentiousness of the classical hero in Hamlet's outburst, above all, in the self-centred quality that makes him imagine that Laertes's genuine expression of grief for Ophelia is merely an attempt to prove his superiority to the prince. Characteristically, the hyperbolic rhetoric which reflects Hamlet's spirited impulse to excel drives him to a classical example. In citing Mount Ossa, the emblem of titanic ambition, he is answering – and outdoing – Laertes's earlier reference to Mount Pelion (V.i.253). When Hamlet's spiritedness is aroused, classical references tend to come easily to his lips:

> My fate cries out
> And makes each petty artere in this body
> As hardy as the Nemean lion's nerve.   (I.iv.81–3)

Such passages do not show that Hamlet is properly under-
stood as a Hercules or an Achilles. But they do suggest that,
contrary to many interpretations, there is an Achillean *side* to
his character. Within the remarkably wide compass of his
soul, he has room for many of the elements of the classical
hero: the pride, the aggressiveness, the capacity for anger and
indignation, the ambition, all the character traits the Greeks
referred to as *thumos*. Hamlet says as much to Ophelia: 'I am
very proud, revengeful, ambitious' (III.i.123–4). He worries
about the dangers of giving vent to his spiritedness:

> Now could I drink hot blood
> And do such bitter business as the day
> Would quake to look on. Soft, now to my mother.
> O heart, lose not thy nature! let not ever
> The soul of Nero enter this firm bosom,
> Let me be cruel, not unnatural;
> I will speak daggers to her, but use none.
> My tongue and soul in this be hypocrites —
> How in my words somever she be shent,
> To give them seals never, my soul, consent!
>
> (III.ii.390–9)

As he vows to drink hot blood, Hamlet comes closer than ever
before to the conventional role of the avenger, taking on a
pagan fierceness. But as he begins to foresee the consequences
of unleashing his spiritedness, he draws back from the prospect. As usual, he thinks of a classical precedent, but this time
it is a cautionary example. He refers, not to a classical hero,
but to the Roman emperor Nero, a case study in the deforma-
tion of *thumos*, of ambition perverted into madness and
destructiveness.

Thus just when Hamlet is beginning to sound as aggressive
and bloodthirsty as any epic warrior, he appeals to the soft,
gentle side of his soul, in order to moderate his fury against
his mother. This speech gives some sense of the forces contend-
ing within his soul, forces set in motion by the contradictory
terms of the ghost's original command. By instructing

Hamlet to pursue his vengeance singlemindedly but under no circumstances to harm his mother, the ghost in fact prevents him from making an absolute commitment to revenge. Faced with the possibility of harming his mother, he cannot afford to unleash violence with the blind fury of Achilles. The savagery of classical heroism must be transformed into something more civilised; Hamlet searches for a metaphorical form of violence ('I will speak daggers to her but use none'). As his talk of hypocrisy suggests, the inhibition of his ability to act opens up the gap between words and deeds which is characteristic of his existence and gives him his distinctive psychological complexity. Thus Hamlet acquires depth as a character precisely because he cannot play the straightforward classical role of the aggressive hero.

I have dwelled at length on those aspects of Shakespeare's portrayal which link Hamlet with the world of classical heroism because many interpreters lose sight of this important dimension and end up with a prince who could not hurt a fly, let alone have a hand in the deaths of half the characters in the play. Still, if Hamlet aspires to be a classical hero, in the world in which he lives he is doomed to be a classical hero *manqué*. He himself senses that he is living in a world of diminished heroic possibilities (V.i.139–41). But the fact that his heroic impulses are denied a direct outlet or an adequate object does not by any means produce a simple diminishment of his being. On the contrary, this kind of frustration in the outer world can be responsible for the development of the inner richness of a soul. It is time, then, to turn to the other side of Hamlet, the side which makes him less heroic in action but more profound in feeling and thought.

Hamlet and Christianity

One might formulate what distinguishes Hamlet from a classical hero in many ways, but one can begin from this basic point: his cosmos is not that of Achilles. The Greek hero lives in a universe with finite horizons: he knows that he is mortal and that death offers at most an existence as a bloodless shade, an existence to which life on earth even as a slave is preferable (as Achilles's shade reveals in the *Odyssey*). His singleminded determination as a warrior is related to his sense of his mortality. Because he knows that his fate is to die young, he realises that he has only a brief period of time to win glory for himself. Indeed, the only meaningful form of immortality his world offers him is the survival of his name through fame.

Hamlet, by contrast, living in the modern Christian world, believes that his soul is immortal (I.iv.65–8). This may seem like an obvious point, but it has wide-ranging implications for our understanding of Shakespeare's play. In fact, it is remarkable how many of the complications of Hamlet's situation can be traced to the impact his belief in an afterlife has on his thinking. From the very beginning he is preoccupied with the afterlife because from the very beginning he is preoccupied with suicide. Suicide is the issue on which Shakespeare demonstrates most clearly his awareness of the distinction between ancient, pagan heroes and modern, Christian ones. From our perspective, suicide is a surprisingly unproblematic notion for Shakespeare's Romans. Their ethic demands suicide from them when dishonour and disgrace are the alternative. Because they view it as a noble deed, they do not hesitate to commit suicide when the time comes. This is true even in the case of Brutus, a character often compared to Hamlet as a thoughtful, meditative man, who has difficulty making up his mind. But Brutus approaches his suicide with a firm resolve. Whatever his temperamental affinities with Hamlet may be, he has a diametrically opposed attitude towards suicide. This difference is not to be explained in terms of what we would today call contrasting 'personalities', but rather in terms of the contrasting regimes under which Brutus and Hamlet live. Brutus's regime virtually mandates suicide for a noble man under certain circumstances, whereas Hamlet's forbids it under any circumstances.

The first words we hear Hamlet speaking alone reveal him running up against the Christian prohibition of suicide:

> O that this too too solid flesh would melt,
> Thaw, and resolve itself into a dew!
> Or that the Everlasting had not fix'd
> His canon 'gainst self-slaughter.   (I.ii.129–32)

These opening lines supply the keynote of Hamlet's character: throughout the play he shows a distinctive concern with the everlasting as opposed to the merely temporal. This orientation means that he cannot view action from the perspective of a classical hero. Unlike Achilles, he must consider whether his actions will lead him to be saved or damned. The fact that an eternity is at stake in his deeds gives him good reason to pause and consider their consequences. But the complications introduced into Hamlet's thinking by his belief in an afterlife run deeper than this. His Christianity opens a window on eternity, but it is a dark window. The most striking fact about the afterlife for Hamlet is that he cannot know with certainty what it will be like. His cosmos is far more mysterious than Achilles's. His belief in the immortality of the soul vastly raises the stakes involved in heroic action but, given the uncertainties surrounding life after death, it simultaneously makes it more difficult to calculate the consequences of such action.

This is the main burden of Hamlet's most famous speech, the 'To be, or not to be' soliloquy. He reveals that he would have no difficulty in embracing suicide if he were a pagan, that is, if he believed that death is effectively the end of life. But he is troubled by visions of what lies beyond the finite horizons to which the ancient world was limited:

> For in that sleep of death what dreams may come
> When we have shuffled off this mortal coil,
> Must give us pause.   (III.i.65–7)

'The dread of something after death' grips Hamlet all the more powerfully because he realises that we must take on faith any claims about 'the undiscovr'd country, from whose bourn / No traveller returns' (III.i.77–9). He dwells on how belief in an afterlife alters the terms of heroic action and threatens to redirect and even stifle heroic impulses:

> thus the native hue of resolution
> Is sicklied o'er with the pale cast of thought,
> And enterprises of great pitch and moment
> With this regard their currents turn awry,
> And lose the name of action.   (III.i.83–7)

Notice that, contrary to the Schlegel–Coleridge thesis, Hamlet does not claim here that thinking as such undermines heroic resolve, but only thinking about a particular subject, namely the afterlife.

Hamlet's other-worldly perspective would complicate his view of any heroic action, but it makes the task of revenge particularly complex. Paradoxically, even while forbidding revenge, Christianity offers a pattern of revenge more sinister than anything imagined in classical antiquity. The statement 'Vengeance is mine, saith the Lord' is in a strange way ambiguous. Though it ostensibly denies man the right to revenge, it simultaneously offers a kind of divine sanction to vengeance by providing a divine model of it. The God of the Old Testament is a vengeful God, and the God of the New, while offering forgiveness to sinners, raises the stakes involved in revenge by damning unrepentant sinners for all eternity. Hamlet's concern for the salvation of his soul makes him more thoughtful and hesitant than a classical hero, but it also means that if he is to take revenge on Claudius, it must be revenge on his immortal soul.

Shakespeare makes this literally the central issue of *Hamlet*. At roughly the middle of the play, at the traditional turning point of the five-act structure, Hamlet has an opportunity to kill Claudius. The king is alone, unguarded, and defenceless, and with the success of the play he stages, Hamlet is finally convinced that the ghost did tell the truth about the murder of his father. If he had killed Claudius at this moment, many if not all of the disasters which later occur might have been avoided. But he refuses to strike out against Claudius because of the situation in which he finds the king:

> Now might I do it pat, now 'a is a-praying;
> And now I'll do it – and so 'a goes to heaven,
> And so am I reveng'd. That would be scann'd:

> A villain kills my father, and for that
> I, his sole son, do this same villain send
> To heaven.
>
> (III.iii.73–8)

At this crucial juncture, Hamlet's religious beliefs intervene to complicate his view of revenge in a peculiarly diabolical manner. He feels that he must act in such a way as to ensure, not just the destruction of Claudius's body, but the damnation of his soul:

> When he is drunk asleep, or in his rage,
> Or in th' incestuous pleasure of his bed,
> At game a-swearing, or about some act
> That has no relish of salvation in't –
> Then trip him, that his heels may kick at heaven
> And that his soul may be as damn'd and black
> As hell, whereto it goes.
>
> (III.iii.89–95)

Hamlet's desire to damn his victim has appalled many interpreters of the play. Samuel Johnson called this speech 'too horrible to be read or to be uttered' (VIII, 990). Coleridge was among the first to argue that what Hamlet says is so repellant that he could not possibly mean it. Coleridge views Hamlet's desire to damn Claudius as merely an excuse for the inaction he has already resolved upon: 'the determination to allow the guilty King to escape at such a moment is only part of the indecision and irresoluteness of the hero. Hamlet seizes hold of a pretext for not acting' (II, 153). Hazlitt similarly claimed that Hamlet's 'refinement in malice' is 'only an excuse for his own want of resolution' (83). Hamlet's refusal to kill Claudius at the opportune moment has thus become a crux for many interpreters of the play. Critics have turned away from his explicitly stated motives in search of hidden reasons for his conduct, such as the Freudian theory of his being caught in an Oedipal bind.

But the fact is that, whatever critics may want Hamlet to be, Shakespeare gave him a long speech at a key moment in which he clearly and vehemently expresses a desire to see his enemy damned in hell. We should not conveniently suppress this evidence, but search for what it can tell us about the prince. In fact, the speech is thoroughly consistent with what

Shakespeare shows about him elsewhere, that the terms of his heroic task have been decisively altered by the Christian context of the action. The task of vengeance becomes more complicated for a man who believes in the immortality of the soul. Some critics have pointed to the dramatic irony of Act III, scene iii. Claudius himself admits that his prayers have been ineffective; presumably, had Hamlet killed him at this moment, his soul would have gone to hell as the prince had hoped. But what critics who fault Hamlet for this reason do not acknowledge is that he has no way of knowing what we as the audience know. Unlike us, he does not hear Claudius's soliloquy: thus he has no reliable access to the King's inner feelings. As the focal point of the action of *Hamlet*, Act III, scene iii dramatises what is distinctive in the world of the play: the new emphasis on the mysterious depths of human interiority that goes hand in hand with the Christian concern for the salvation of souls. Achilles has no interest in what is going on in Hector's soul when he exacts vengeance for Patroclus. But as Hamlet views the world, the success of his revenge hinges entirely on the state of Claudius's soul at the moment he kills him. But since he can never have any objective evidence of whether the king's soul goes to heaven or to hell, everything comes to hinge on his ability to spy into Claudius's soul, which is to say, on his ability to interpret the state of his inner feelings. That Hamlet in fact misinterprets these feelings in Act III, scene iii is one indication of how his religious beliefs have introduced a new complexity into his possibilities for acting heroically.

Fortunately, to raise the question of Hamlet's religious beliefs need not involve us in the thorny question of Shakespeare's. Though many critics have presumed to speak for Shakespeare on the issue of religion, it is extremely difficult – if not impossible – to construct a consistent religious doctrine out of his plays. But we can reasonably examine the religious sentiments which Shakespeare attributes to individual characters within his plays without thereby identifying these sentiments as Shakespeare's. Indeed, as a general point, what I have been trying to show is that

Shakespeare characterises his figures not simply in terms of what we might call their temperaments or personalities, but in terms of their opinions or beliefs or, more broadly, their views of the cosmos. We have seen that in considering basic questions about Hamlet such as: why does he not commit suicide or why does he not kill Claudius when he has the chance?, we must take into account his Christian belief in an afterlife. (Whether in the way he applies this belief Hamlet is behaving as a *good* Christian is very much open to dispute, but that his beliefs are those of a Christian as opposed to a pagan cannot be denied.) The complexity of Hamlet's stated view of the world − and above all the way it brings together classical and Christian elements in an uneasy fusion − may well be responsible for the fact that he cannot respond to the ghost's challenge in a simple and direct way.

Shakespeare's attention to the religious beliefs of his characters is evident in the care with which he differentiates them. For example, Horatio's distinctive set of beliefs helps to highlight Hamlet's. As his name indicates, there is something Roman about Horatio. This is, typically, most evident in his attitude towards suicide. When he tries to follow Hamlet in death, he explicitly views it as a pagan act: 'I am more an antique Roman than a Dane' (V.ii.341). When Hamlet discusses the qualities he admires in Horatio, he presents him in terms that call to mind a Roman Stoic (III.ii.63–74). Horatio's Romanness is related to a certain religious skepticism he displays. He is the one character to express doubts about the ghost:

> Horatio says 'tis but our fantasy,
> And will not let belief take hold of him.   (I.i.23–4)

He refuses to take anything on hearsay and does not accept the fact of the ghost until he sees it with his own eyes (I. i.56–8). Even after experiencing the apparition, he refuses to give full assent to Marcellus's conventionally pious report of beliefs about ghosts; Horatio replies: 'So have I heard and do in part believe it' (I. i. 165).

The fact that rational skepticism seems to be the keynote

of Horatio's character may explain why Hamlet feels compelled
to distinguish his philosophical position from his friend's:

> There are more things in heaven and earth, Horatio,
> Than are dreamt of in your philosophy. (I.v.166–7)

Like many commentators, Harold Jenkins glosses these lines
thus: 'not some particular philosophy of Horatio's but
philosophy in general, *your* being used in the indefinite sense
then common' (226). This reading may be correct (and is
perhaps supported by the fact that the Folio reading at this
point is 'our philosophy'). But given the fact that these lines
are pointedly directed at Horatio by name, they would be
more forceful if Hamlet did have in mind specifically just that
skeptical tendency we have seen Shakespeare portraying as
characteristic of Horatio. We do not have to imagine the two
friends staying up all night at Wittenberg engrossed in
metaphysical disputations to see that Shakespeare is trying to
discriminate among his characters. The skepticism of the
would-be Roman Horatio serves as a foil to the broader
metaphysical horizons of Hamlet. Whereas Horatio has had
his skepticism merely shaken by the appearance of the ghost,
for Hamlet it has shattered the boundaries of the finite world
and awakened in him 'thoughts beyond the reaches of our
souls' (I.iv.56).

Hamlet's metaphysical quarrel with Horatio gives an inkling
of those aspects of his view of the world which work against
his heroic impulses. Heroic action begins to lose some of its
lustre when viewed from the perspective of eternity. For all
his admiration for classical antiquity, Hamlet has a distinctly
Christian sense of the transiency of the glory of the ancient
world. He even sounds like a preacher in the way he imagines
the nobility of Alexander the Great reduced to dust. (Horatio
cautions against the unsettling effects of this outlook:
' 'Twere to consider too curiously, to consider so', V.i.205–6.)
Hamlet measures the greatest of ancient heroes against the
Christian standard of eternity and finds them wanting:

> Imperious Caesar, dead and turn'd to clay,
> Might stop a hole to keep the wind away.

> O that that earth which kept the world in awe
> Should patch a wall t'expel the winter's flaw!   (V.i.213–16)

He reads the same lesson of the brittleness of earthly glory in the fate of his father's reputation in Denmark:

> O heaven, die two months ago, and not forgotten yet? Then there's hope a great man's memory may outlive his life half a year.
> (III.ii.130–2)

Related to Hamlet's concern with eternal as opposed to temporal things is a certain cosmopolitanism in his outlook. His mind is so wide-ranging and comprehensive that he finds it difficult to take Denmark and Danish affairs seriously. Though as a prince he ought to uphold the customs of his country, he in fact despises them and is willing to say so in conversation with Horatio about the king's drinking ceremony:

> *Horatio*   Is it a custom?
> *Hamlet*   Ay, marry, is't.
>   But to my mind, though I am native here
>   And to the manner born, it is a custom
>   More honor'd in the breach than the observance.
>   This heavy-headed revel east and west
>   Makes us traduc'd and tax'd of other nations.
>   They clip us drunkards, and with swinish phrase
>   Soil our addition.   (I.iv.12–20)

Hamlet's awareness of what other nations think of Denmark is in itself an admirable quality. His willingness to agree with foreign criticism of his countrymen shows the independence and integrity of his mind. But it also means that when Hamlet is called upon to purify Denmark, he will be less likely to believe that the task is worthwhile or even possible.

Shakespeare went out of his way to portray Denmark as a kind of cultural backwater in Europe. As *Hamlet* opens, both Laertes and Hamlet are asking permission to leave the country for more interesting locales, such as Paris and Wittenberg. One can get a measure of Hamlet's feeling for his native land by the fact that he tends to greet old friends with the question: 'What are you doing here?', with the implication 'when you

could be somewhere more interesting'. The players who arrive
at Claudius's court, far from rejoicing in an opportunity for
a royal command performance, seem to view it as a kind
of theatrical exile. Playing even at the court of Denmark
apparently is regarded by the actors as being condemned to
the provinces.

Hamlet is deeply disturbed by the provinciality of Denmark. He feels hemmed in, unable to give free rein to the
expansive impulses of his spirit. But the problem is not simply
with Denmark:

Hamlet   What have you, my good friends, deserv'd at the
                hands of Fortune, that she sends you to prison hither?
Guildenstern Prison, my lord?
Hamlet   Denmark's a prison.
Rosencrantz Then is the world one.
Hamlet   A goodly one, in which there are many confines,
                wards, and dungeons, Denmark being one o' th' worst.
                                                        (II.ii.239–47)

Hamlet has reason to believe that Denmark is particularly
confining, but ultimately he feels imprisoned and disgusted
by the world itself:

> How weary, stale, flat, and unprofitable
> Seem to me all the uses of this world!   (I.ii.133–4)

Hamlet's *contemptus mundi* attitude is perhaps the most
Christian aspect of his character and certainly the one most
in tension with his admiration for classical heroism. Unlike a
classical hero, he does not feel at home in this world. Far
from believing that this world is all man has, he is haunted
by visions of a world beyond.

Moreover, unlike a classical hero, Hamlet has a brooding
sense that the appearances of this world conceal a deeper
reality. That is why the world is so much more mysterious to
him than it is to Achilles or Aeneas. He lives in a world in
which the truth seems covered by veil after veil, and in which
men must resort to devious methods to spy it out (Polonius
says 'By indirections find directions out', II.i.63). Hamlet's
disillusioning experiences – especially watching his mother
betray the memory of his father – have led him to distrust

appearances. Characteristically his first speech in the play expresses his contempt for seeming and his suspicion that truth lies buried beneath layers of deception (I.ii.76–86). His conviction that 'customary suits of solemn black' cannot express the truth of mourning reflects that general distrust of custom we saw in his attitude towards Denmark.

Hamlet is particularly disturbed by the customs of women, which call forth his most bitter and cynical remarks. Their habitual use of cosmetics symbolises for him the duplicity of the human world:

> I have heard of your paintings, well enough. God hath given you one face, and you make yourselves another.   (III.i.142–4)

His obsession with women's makeup culminates in his instructions to Yorick's skull:

> Now get you to my lady's chamber, and tell her, let her paint an inch thick, to this favor she must come; make her laugh at that.
>   (V.i.192–5)

The movement of this speech is characteristic of the way Hamlet's mind works: he takes fair appearances and strips away their outer layers until something ugly comes into view. The cosmos itself is not immune to his corrosive vision:

> this goodly frame, the earth, seems to me a sterile promontory; this most excellent canopy, the air, look you, this brave o'erhanging firmament, this majestical roof fretted with golden fire, why, it appeareth nothing to me but a foul and pestilent congregation of vapors.   (II.ii.298–303)

Faith in the heroic potentiality of humanity has a hard time withstanding this kind of questioning. To Hamlet a courtier is merely 'spacious in the possession of dirt' (V.ii.87–8) and man himself, seemingly 'the beauty of the world; the paragon of animals', is reduced to a 'quintessence of dust' (II.ii.307–8).

Hamlet is thus characterised by a kind of absolutism. One can see this in the way he idealises the memory of his father into an image of perfection. *Infinite* is one of his favourite words (I.iv.34, II.ii.255, 304; V.i.186). He has a kind of all-or-nothing attitude: if the world or people do not live up to his image of perfection, they are worthless to him. Thus, the

more idealistic his view of heroism becomes, the less likely it
is that any concrete act of heroism can satisfy him. The complexity of his attitude towards heroism can be seen in his near-
encounter with Fortinbras in Act IV. Of all the characters in
Hamlet, Fortinbras comes closest to embodying the old-style
heroism. Hamlet genuinely responds to his example; he is
struck by the Norwegian's courage and reproaches himself
for not displaying a similar heroic resolve. But even as he
celebrates the ambitious spirit of Fortinbras, Hamlet cannot
fail to see the limited range of the goals he pursues. In Fortinbras's campaign against Poland, Hamlet is confronted by an
image of what deeply disturbs him: the paradoxical yoking of
the infinity of human aspiration with the finitude of its
objects. However grand Fortinbras's heroic impulses may be,
Hamlet learns that they are directed towards a very finite
piece of property:

> Truly to speak, and with no addition,
> We go to gain a little patch of ground
> That hath in it no profit but the name.
> To pay five ducats, five, I would not farm it.
>
> (IV.iv.17–21)

Thus Hamlet's reaction to Fortinbras becomes profoundly
ambivalent: he tries to take inspiration from the Norwegian's
example, but cannot help seeing through the illusion of his
greatness:

> Examples gross as earth exhort me:
> Witness this army of such mass and charge,
> Led by a delicate and tender prince,
> Whose spirit with divine ambition puff'd,
> Makes mouths at the invisible event,
> Exposing what is mortal and unsure
> To all that fortune, death, and danger dare,
> Even for an egg-shell.   (IV.iv.46–53)

With his heroic rhetoric, Hamlet inflates the balloon of Fortinbras's greatness, only to pop it himself with one common-
place word: *egg-shell*. In this speech we can see the contradictory impulses in Hamlet's soul at work. On the one hand,
there is his admiration for martial virtue, his classical sense

that 'ambition' is 'divine', his longing for an epic brand of heroism. On the other hand, there is his refusal to accept heroic action at face value, his probing beneath the surface issues of epic warfare to reveal the triviality of the disputes at its base, his suspicion that the heroic warrior is merely deceiving himself and throwing away his life and many others for the sake of an empty ideal. Just when Hamlet finally has a concrete example of heroism before his eyes, it turns out to be too concrete: he recognises how finite and transient the objects of this heroism are, and from Hamlet's eternal perspective as a Christian, all this earthly glory shrinks to the dimensions of an eggshell.

At the heart of Hamlet's experience of Fortinbras's campaign is his perception of the disjunction between the subjective feeling of heroic action and its objective meaning:

> Rightly to be great
> Is not to stir without great argument,
> But greatly to find quarrel in a straw
> When honor's at the stake. (IV.iv.53–6)

Hamlet's doubts about heroism are chiefly focused on the inadequacy of the object to the heroic impulse. It is ironic, then, that the one time within the play when he strikes out with the impulsiveness of an epic hero, he does so in total ignorance of the object of his wrath. The way he murders Polonius – striking blindly through a curtain – is strangely emblematic of his whole situation. He is called upon to act heroically, but, unlike a classical hero, he is denied clear knowledge of the meaning of heroic action. When the elder Hamlet fought the elder Fortinbras, they stood face-to-face: each knew who his opponent was, and what they were fighting for. But in *Hamlet* everything happens, as it were, 'through a glass darkly', or rather 'through an arras darkly'. We tend to think of classical heroes fighting out their battles in broad daylight and in clear view of the public. But in *Hamlet*, much of the action takes place at night, deliberately hidden from public view, steeped in the deep secrecy of treachery.

Hamlet's doubts about the veracity of the ghost are only

one example of the uncertainties which surround all his attempts at action. When he tries to act heroically in Act III, scene iv, he literally does not know what he is doing. The larger context of his action is obscure to him. In this sense, the murder of Polonius prefigures the final scene of the play, when Hamlet again can only blunder into acting heroically. In what is an even more pointed contrast to the original Hamlet–Fortinbras combat, the prince finally accomplishes his revenge and dies in a profoundly ambiguous action: a game that is not really a game, a battle that is not really a battle, fighting against an opponent who is not his true opponent, in a cause that is not his true cause. Taking a cue from this final scene, we may say that in *Hamlet* the atmosphere of heroic action has been poisoned. In this situation in which, to use the words of Macbeth (I.iii.140–2), 'nothing is / But what is not', it is no wonder that for Hamlet 'function / Is smother'd in surmise.'

Hamlet as tragic hero

Analysing the classical and the Christian strains in Hamlet's character reveals the complexity of Shakespeare's portrayal, a complexity which mirrors the richness of the Renaissance itself. Hamlet is uniquely situated to bring out this richness of the age, standing as he does at the intersection of disparate worlds. Shakespeare portrays him as a cultivated and sophisticated product of modern Christian Europe, who is suddenly asked to step out of a university classroom and into a situation ultimately derived from the barbaric world of Norse saga. Thus what makes Hamlet the quintessential tragic figure of the Renaissance is that the inner contradictions of the era come to consciousness in his alert and capacious mind. He is usually viewed as self-divided, but many critics treat his self-division as a kind of pathological state, as if the community Hamlet lives in were whole and only he fragmented. But his self-division reflects a more fundmental division in his age. Indeed Hamlet is distinguished in the play precisely by the fact that only he is truly aware of the contradictions in his era.

The symbolic geography of *Hamlet* mirrors the interplay of forces that went to make up the Renaissance. Shakespeare's Denmark is a kind of borderland, lying on the fringes of modern Europe, halfway between the old world of pagan heroism and the new world of Christian civility. To the north stands Norway, a yet untamed world of 'lawless resolutes' (I.i.98). Associated with the struggle of the elder Hamlet and the elder Fortinbras, Norway conjures up images of single combat between martial heroes. It is presented in the play as a kind of Homeric realm surviving on the frontiers of modern civilization. Out of this world comes the younger Fortinbras, and with him whatever remains of the old-style heroism in *Hamlet*.

To the south of Denmark lies the heart of modern Europe, cultivated cities like Paris, an unheroic world in which men learn to fence rather than to smite 'the sledded Polacks on the ice' (I.i.63). As Laertes's attraction to the city shows, Paris is associated with new fashions of all kinds, from the latest style of dress (I.iii.72–4) to the newest forms of entertainment and sport (including, for example, tennis, II.i.57, and falconry, II.ii.430). Claudius holds up a Norman named Lamord as a model of gentlemanliness and chivalry for Laertes: 'this gallant' (IV.vii.84) is the sort of man who educates the wandering youths of Denmark. The Danes also head south for their education to Wittenberg, a university town, associated in Shakespeare's day with both Doctor Faustus and Martin Luther, and hence with the new intellectual and religious currents of both the Renaissance and the Reformation.

Thus, as he often does in his tragedies, Shakespeare places his hero at the crossroads of a divided world. Shakespeare's Denmark is to the northern borders of Europe what his Cyprus is to the southern. In the symbolic geography of *Othello*, Cyprus stands midway between the Christian civilisation of Venice and the pagan barbarism of the Turkish Empire, and thus is the appropriate setting for the tragedy of Othello, who is caught between these two worlds. Hamlet's geographical situation similarly reflects the range of ethical alternatives available to him. Placed as it were halfway between Norway and Paris, he is able to look beyond the borders of his country and in effect to survey the history of Western culture, to see its competing models of human excellence in the figures who surround him. There is Laertes, the model of a modern courtier, a young gallant trained in Paris. There is Hamlet's fellow student, Horatio, schooled at Wittenberg in Stoic ideas, and a model of rational control. And finally there is Fortinbras, Hamlet's Norwegian model of the heroic soldier. Hamlet can find something to admire in all these models, but he can also see the limitations of each, partly because he measures one against the others. Precisely because he is open to all of them, he never becomes the captive of any single model. As a result, the other characters in the play seem one-dimensional by comparison with Hamlet. Next to him, Laertes seems superficial and callow, Horatio cold and unfeeling, and Fortinbras rash and narrow-minded. Comparing Hamlet to Laertes, Horatio and Fortinbras reminds us that one's 'geographic situation' is not in itself enough to generate tragedy. These characters are after all placed roughly in the same locale as Hamlet and yet they do not become tragic heroes. The reason is that they do not share his openness to the ethical alternatives this world offers.

Hamlet's is thus a peculiar form of heroism: rather than pursuing one heroic model to an extreme, he moves back and forth between a number of competing heroic models, subjecting them all in the process to a critique. What makes Hamlet stand out in his world is thus not a traditional greatness of soul, but the largeness of his horizons, his heightened awareness of all that his complex culture contains and the depth and authenticity of his response to its contradictory ethical demands. His soul itself becomes a kind of crossroads, a battleground on which pagan and Christian, ancient and modern values meet and fight to a standstill, leaving Hamlet unable to remain true to any one ethic and thus unable to accomplish what his concrete situation demands of him. From the very beginning, he is faced with an impossible task: to exact a barbaric pagan vengeance with the tenderness of a civilised Christian. To accomplish this goal, he would have to be a kind of Nietzschean superman: 'the Roman Caesar with Christ's soul' (*The Will to Power*, sect. 983). If Hamlet ultimately fails to achieve his revenge within the constraints laid down by his father's ghost, his failure results from a kind of overreaching, and thus is tragic.

There is, then, a connection between Hamlet's being what we would call a Renaissance man and his being a tragic hero. Ophelia may exaggerate when she attributes to him 'the courtier's, soldier's, scholar's, eye, tongue, sword' (III.i.151), but she is correct in sensing that he tries to embrace all sides of life. He seems in fact at times to wish to be all things to all people. Though a prince by birth, he prides himself on his practical knowledge of the theatre and the way he can talk to the players on familiar terms and in their own language. As we have seen in his confrontation with Laertes over Ophelia's grave, Hamlet vows to outdo Laertes in any part he chooses to play: mourner, fighter, ascetic. With his quick wit, verbal facility, and theatrical talent, he can shine in many roles. But the inner richness which allows him to play such a wealth of parts works against him when he has to settle down to the singleminded task of pursuing vengeance. He does not have the kind of one-track mind revenge requires. A simpler man would have either rejected the task of vengeance or embraced it wholeheartedly and in a more direct form.

One might attempt a formulation of Hamlet's tragedy this way: precisely because of his comprehensiveness of outlook, the way he follows the Renaissance ideal of trying to combine disparate ethics, he exposes the profound tensions between those ethics, ending up in a tragic situation in which his own principles make contradictory demands upon him and hence paralyse him. The positive side of Hamlet's cosmopolitanism is that he is open to all the diverse influences the modern world has to offer. Its negative side is that precisely that diversity of influences prevents him from ever playing a simple role with utter conviction. One can see this problem in one of his most distinctive characteristics, his theatrical self-consciousness. Hamlet can respond emotionally to the appeal of his father's ghost, and part of him clearly wants to wreak vengeance on Claudius. There are moments when he seems enthusiastically to embrace a heroic role and even his Danish heritage, as, for example, in his appearance at Ophelia's grave: 'This is I, / Hamlet the Dane!' (V.i.257–8). But one detects more than a hint of irony in the way Hamlet here announces himself. He seems to be deliberately overacting the part, spurred into competition by Laertes's histrionic outbursts of grief over Ophelia.

Even in his moments of passion, Hamlet maintains a critical detachment that prevents him from ever completely plunging into the role his circumstances dictate. He is governed in his life by the principle of acting which he articulates to the troupe of players: 'in the very torrent, tempest, and, as I may say, whirlwind of your passion, you must acquire and beget a temperance that may give it smoothness' (III.ii.5–8). This may be a good principle of acting on the stage, but it may not be a good principle of acting in the real world. In a play, one needs to be in control of one's passions, but when performing real deeds, one often needs the impulsion of genuine passions. Hamlet continually hesitates to act because he will not allow himself to be swept away by his passions. His intellect is constantly leading him to deny meaning to the very acts he feels impelled to perform. He is supposed to right the wrongs in his native land, and yet he has nothing but contempt for Denmark. He is supposed to uphold his father's honor, and yet his study of history has shown him that political reputations are arbitrarily won and seldom long maintained. Above all, he is supposed to take action in this world, and yet he is constantly haunted by visions of the next, which threaten to make earthly life pale into insignificance for him.

The end of *Hamlet*

The genuine complexity of Hamlet's tragic situation means that the resolution of the plot does not offer a simple resolution of his ethical dilemma. Many critics have tried to portray the conclusion of *Hamlet* as more positive than it really is, thereby blunting the force of Shakespeare's tragedy. These critics point to a demonstrable change in the prince's mood in Act V. Having escaped Claudius's plot against his life, he seems to have a renewed faith in divine providence:

> There's a divinity that shapes our ends,
> Rough-hew them how we will.   (V.ii.10–11)

As the final confrontation with Claudius approaches, Hamlet has a sense of resignation about his fate:

We defy augury. There is special providence in the fall of a sparrow. If it be now, 'tis not to come; if it be not to come, it will be now; if it be not now, yet it will come — the readiness is all. Since no man, of aught he leaves, knows what is't to leave betimes, let be.

                                                  (V.ii.219–24)

There is something attractive and soothing about these speeches, and critics are understandably relieved to see a calm descending upon the hitherto tormented Hamlet. Yet only a few lines before this speech, he is still saying to Horatio:

Thou wouldst not think how ill all's here about my heart — but it is no matter.   (V.ii.212–13)

As these words reveal, there is a strong element of indifference in Hamlet's resignation. His sense of providence may in fact be a new example of how his religious beliefs interfere with his efficacy as an avenger.

For the fact is that Hamlet's new sense of providence has not given him a new sense of purpose. Though he is more than ever convinced of his duty to kill Claudius, he is no closer to having a concrete plan for doing so. When he talks of his 'readiness', he is referring merely to his willingness to play a reactive role, and as events unfold in Act V, it is clear that he is allowing Claudius once again to take the initiative in their struggle. The new Hamlet of Act V is a fatalist, convinced that nothing he can do will alter the outcome of events if God wills otherwise. Far from sharpening his sense of his ethical position, then, his faith in providence actually blurs it. The Hamlet of Act V is less willing to take responsibility for his actions than the Hamlet we see earlier in the play, who reproaches himself in soliloquies for failing to heed the

ghost's command. By contrast, in excusing his conduct to
Laertes in Act V, he resorts to a form of casuistry to separate
himself from his deeds:

> Was't Hamlet wrong'd Laertes? Never Hamlet!
> If Hamlet from himself be ta'en away,
> And when he's not himself does wrong Laertes,
> Then Hamlet does it not, Hamlet denies it.
> Who does it then? His madness. (V.ii.233–7)

Hamlet's diminished sense of ethical responsibility is a
dangerous tendency. His fatalistic feelings about his struggle
with Claudius are after all what allowed him to send the
relatively innocent Rosencrantz and Guildenstern to their
'sudden death, / Not shriving time allow'd', and claim a clear
conscience about the deed (V.ii.46–7, 58).

In short, we need to evaluate the Hamlet of Act V, not just
by the sentiments of his speeches, but by the consequences of
his deeds as well. To read some accounts of the end of the
play, one would think that with his faith in providence,
Hamlet finally finds a way to resolve all his problems and accomplish his revenge in a fully satisfactory manner. He does
finally kill Claudius, but at a terrible cost. One need only
measure his achievement against the original terms of the
ghost's command to see how catastrophic the ending of the
play is. Hamlet was not supposed to harm his mother, and yet
by the end of the play she lies dead. He was not supposed to
taint his mind, and yet by the end of the play he has the blood
of Polonius, Rosencrantz, Guildenstern and Laertes on his
hands. By not trying to shape the course of events but rather
merely responding to Claudius's maneouvers, Hamlet does
destroy his enemy, but in the process ends up destroying
much that is good in Denmark as well, including himself.

Hamlet's conduct in the final act might even be interpreted
as a form of suicide. From the beginning of the play his great
frustration is that his religion forbids suicide. But in Act V
Hamlet finally finds a way to be killed without having to take
responsibility for the deed himself. This variation on the
theme of suicide is explored by the clownish gravediggers,
who in their efforts to excuse Ophelia, come up with the

paradoxical notion that 'she drown'd herself in her own defense' (V.i.6–7). The grave-diggers articulate what later emerges as the principle of Hamlet's suicidal non-suicide:

Here lies the water; good. Here stands the man; good. If the man go to this water and drown himself, it is, will he, nill he, he goes, mark you that. But if the water come to him and drown him, he drowns not himself; argal, he that is not guilty of his own death shortens not his own life. (V.i.15–20)

Employing the kind of casuistry Hamlet uses with Laertes, the gravediggers appear to be giving a proleptic defence of his conduct in the final scene: 'If Claudius invites Hamlet to the fatal fencing match, rather than Hamlet inviting Claudius, then the prince is not guilty of his own death.'

Hamlet does seem to be in need of some kind of defence. His behaviour in the final scene is at the very least imprudent. He lets himself be goaded into a fencing match staged by his bitterest enemy, a man he knows to be treacherous and fond of diabolical machinations. At one point he even appears to suspect treachery, when he questions the equality of the foils, perhaps because he has noticed Laertes's eagerness to get one particular weapon (V.ii.264–5). But by this point, Hamlet's original world-weariness and his new-found fatalism have combined to make him eager to see everything over and done with, by whatever means and at whatever cost, even his own life. He finally is willing to do what the ghost wants and kill Claudius, but only when he can simultaneously accomplish his own deepest purpose and die in the process. Viewed from this perspective, his fatalism in Act V is not a correction of, or an advance beyond, his world-weariness in the earlier acts but only its logical extension.

In their eagerness to find something positive in the ending of *Hamlet*, some critics point to the political resolution. They argue that Hamlet does eventually set things right in Denmark by offering his people a new king in the person of Fortinbras, who has been portrayed positively as a heroic leader throughout the play. Presumably, by taking charge of the situation in Denmark and restoring order, Fortinbras is supposed to provide a neat resolution to the conflicts the play has uncovered. Unfortunately for this interpretation, the Fortinbras we have come to know seems ill-suited to the role of reconciler in Denmark. Though Hamlet admires Fortinbras for his courage, the general impression of him in the play is more negative. He is in fact presented as a troublemaker; his own uncle does everything he can to keep him out of Norway and direct his spiritedness against Poland. Even Hamlet has to admit that Fortinbras's Polish expedition will waste the lives of thousands of men, thereby calling into question the warrior's political judgement.

Moreover, even if Fortinbras were presented as a purely admirable political figure, he has one decided point against him as a potential king of Denmark: he is a Norwegian. It is a final sign of Hamlet's cosmopolitanism that in his dying words he recommends a foreigner for the throne of his homeland. His rising above local prejudice may be a remarkable trait, but his apparent indifference to the basic political distinction between *us* and *them* shows how little he really understands politics. To be sure, there are situations in which a nation might be prepared to welcome a foreigner as king. English history offers several examples: indeed, shortly after *Hamlet* appeared, James VI of Scotland was to succeed Queen Elizabeth on the English throne. But in such cases, the accession of a foreigner was always viewed as in itself problematic, and only overwhelming political necessity dictated resorting to this solution. In James's case, the fact that he was a Protestant rather than a Catholic counted far more than the fact that he was Scottish rather than English. No such case is established for Fortinbras in *Hamlet*. We do not get a chance to see how the Danish people react to the prospect of a Norwegian on their throne. But we can say that the difference between Danes and Norwegians is taken very seriously in the body of the play. From the very first scene, the focus of Danish politics has been the effort to frustrate Norwegian designs on Denmark. The play begins with an account of the elder Hamlet's triumph over the elder Fortinbras, which increased Denmark's power *vis-à-vis* Norway. As the action unfolds, we learn that Denmark is now fighting to prevent the younger Fortinbras from overturning the elder Hamlet's political accomplishment. Claudius does not have the elder Hamlet's heroic power to protect Denmark, but he does employ shrewd diplomacy to hold the younger Fortinbras in check.

In his last moments, Hamlet seems willing to throw this policy to the winds. He wants to hand the Danish throne over to a Norwegian, specifically the son of his own father's greatest antagonist. What the Norwegians could not win by invasion, Hamlet will hand them by invitation. This seems to be Shakespeare's addition to the story: there is no precedent for this action in any of the sources we have for *Hamlet* (that is, no parallel can be found in either Saxo Grammaticus or Belleforest; whether the Fortinbras episode was present in the *Ur-Hamlet* we may never know). The only parallel is to be found in the peculiar analogue to *Hamlet*, the German play *Der bestrafte Brudermord* ('Fratricide Punished', first published in 1781 from a manuscript dated 1710). The exact relation of this text to *Hamlet* is hard to determine; when scholars first became aware of it in the late eighteenth century, some hoped they had found a text ultimately derived from the *Ur-Hamlet*, but the best contemporary critical opinion suggests that *Der bestrafte Brudermord* is instead a very corrupt descendant of some version of Shakespeare's *Hamlet*. In any case, the German play concludes with Hamlet saying: 'Gentle Horatio, take the crown to my cousin, Duke Fortenbras of Norway, so that the kingdom may not fall into other hands' (Bullough, VII, 158). In keeping with the way this much truncated version simplifies the story and tries to clear up its mysteries, Hamlet is here given a simple and comprehensible motive for naming Fortinbras to the throne, a motive which even sounds patriotic. The German Hamlet wants to keep the crown in the family. But Shakespeare's version does not contain the slightest hint of any kinship between Hamlet and Fortinbras. When the Norwegian speaks of 'some rights, of memory in this kingdom' (V.ii.389), he is presumably referring to his claim to the lands his father lost to Hamlet's father. The German version thus highlights how dubious Hamlet's choice of Fortinbras for the throne of

Denmark is in Shakespeare's version. Hamlet's final action in the last scene seems in fact to undo everything his father was said to have accomplished in the first.

The political resolution of the plot of *Hamlet* thus hardly offers evidence for a positive reading of the end of the play. If anything, the prospect of Denmark falling into Norwegian hands should increase our sense of hollowness and futility at the end. It is a deeply ironic moment, and Fortinbras's emergence as king is at best an equivocal triumph for Denmark, if not an outright political defeat. But we should in any case be wary of efforts to impose a happy ending on *Hamlet*, efforts which tend to trivialise the hero's tragedy. To read some critics, one would think that *Hamlet* is some kind of religious homily, and that all its hero had to do was learn a few Christian truths and all his problems were over. But, as we have seen, Hamlet's Christianity is precisely one of the chief complicating factors in his situation, and right up to the end of the play it prevents him from acting efficaciously as an avenger. Reading other critics, one would think that the ending of the play suggests that the restoration of order under Fortinbras somehow makes up for the convulsions Denmark has gone through, and that, however tragic Hamlet's death may be, he died in a good cause. But an order that can come about only through the death of Hamlet is deeply flawed and suspect.

In the end, it is surprising how many interpretations of *Hamlet* somehow lose sight of the fact that the play is a tragedy. Without fully realising the implications of what they are doing, many critics discuss Hamlet as if there were in fact some way out of his dilemma. But if we concentrate on the tragic conflict between the classical and Christian elements in Hamlet, we can see that no resolution of his problem is possible. This may strike some as an oversimplification of Hamlet's situation, and I must confess that, having analysed the play as best I can, I still feel that a sense of mystery remains, that no explanation can cover all the questions *Hamlet* raises. Nevertheless, I believe that if Hamlet remains a mystery, the conflict between the classical and Christian elements in his story stands at the centre of that mystery. If this seems like a simplistic account of *Hamlet*, I would answer that it may be a simple formulation of the prince's tragedy, but it is not a formulation of a simple tragedy. The conflict between the classical and the Christian traditions has been central to Western civilisation, and has provided the basis for both its profoundest cultural achievements and its most deeply problematic moments. That *Hamlet* reflects these tensions, which reached their peak during the Renaissance, is one reason for the enduring power of the play.

Chapter 3

Dramatic and poetic technique

The drama of *Hamlet*

In analysing the tragic conflict in *Hamlet*, one may lose sight of its sheer brilliance as a piece of theatre. The play has fascinated critics searching for the secret of the hero's delay, but it has also thrilled audiences with the twists and turns of its plot, as well as the soaring flights of its poetry. When one discusses the complexities of the play's meaning, one risks giving the impression that it would be 'caviary to the general' (II.ii.437), too complex and subtle for the average audience to appreciate. But in fact, in terms of number of performances and audience response, *Hamlet* must be one of the most successful plays ever written. Its greatness may ultimately rest on the profundity of its portrayal of the tragic reality of the Renaissance, but we must not forget that an integral part of Shakespeare's achievement was to dramatise that tragedy.

In analysing the dramatic structure of *Hamlet*, I will discuss it on the model of the traditional five-act play. I realise the difficulties with this approach; the division of the play into acts and scenes has been supplied by modern editors, and thus we have no certainty that it corresponds to Shakespeare's intentions. The Second Quarto has no act and scene divisions; the Folio marks off only I.i, I.ii, I.iii, II, and II.ii. In my analysis, I will use the standard act and scene divisions, even though a few have with some legitimacy been challenged. But in any event, my argument will not rest on any of the details of the act and scene divisions (and I do not wish to imply anything about Shakespeare's general principles of dramatic construction or his methods of composition); all I am claiming is that the overall dramatic movement of *Hamlet* can best be described in terms of the traditional pattern of the five-act play.

In a five-act structure, Act I is devoted to exposition, and the first act of *Hamlet* does an excellent job of introducing us to the cast of characters and laying the foundation of a dramatic conflict. As critics since Coleridge have noted, the first scene is a particular masterpiece of exposition. The situation of soldiers on guard in a country fearing foreign invasion makes it quite natural for someone to fill in the political background to the present troubles in Denmark. The way the ghost is introduced makes the scene especially effective on the stage. In an atmosphere of vague foreboding, the ghost is referred to at first only in the most abstract and general terms; Marcellus asks: 'What, has this thing appear'd again to-night?' (I.i.21). Only gradually do we begin to get a fuller picture of what is troubling the characters on stage. We learn first that the nameless, unspecified 'thing' is some 'dreaded sight' and then more specifically that it is an 'apparition' (I.i.25, 28). But before we are told anything more, the ghost itself appears in the awesome image of the dead King Hamlet. The fact that the ghost refuses to speak serves to increase the sense of suspense and dread at the opening of the play. One would be hard pressed to think of a scene more perfectly calculated to draw an audience into a play.

After establishing an ominous and mysterious atmosphere in the first scene, Shakespeare introduces us to the Danish court in the second. Presented in a solemn and ceremonial moment, the court seems to be functioning more effectively than we might have surmised from what we learned in the opening scene. Claudius appears to be a competent and even dignified monarch, secure in his control of the court. Shakespeare went out of his way to create Claudius as a worthy antagonist for Hamlet. He could have portrayed Claudius as a standard stage villain, perhaps as an overbearing tyrant or a snivelling coward. But instead Shakespeare created a Claudius who does a convincing job of playing the role of a king, giving at least the appearance of being concerned for his country and his family, including his nephew-son, Hamlet. As critics, we have become so familiar with *Hamlet* that we sometimes must make an effort to resist reading the early scenes in light of the later and attempt to recover a sense of how the play unfolds for a first-time viewer. One source of the dramatic tension Shakespeare creates is the gap between the appearance Claudius gives of being a good king and the secret knowledge of his crime we come to share with Hamlet. Indeed, strictly speaking, it is not until Claudius's aside at III.i.48–53 that we as audience can be sure that the ghost was telling the truth about Claudius.

In the midst of the Danish court − colourful with its elaborate costumes and other trappings of state − Shakespeare reveals the dark, brooding figure of Hamlet, dressed in black and thus set off from the crowd on stage. Shakespeare further emphasises Hamlet's isolation by giving him a distinct manner of speech, above all, the puns with which he replies to Claudius (I. ii.65–7), as well as the tortured poetry of his first soliloquy. *Hamlet* is a play built up in baroque fashion out of sharp and often startling contrasts: first Hamlet pitted against the other characters, then within Hamlet himself, an often bizarre sense of humor pitted against a heartache and a profound sense of misery that breaks out in his soliloquies.

In the third scene of Act I, Shakespeare begins to develop the characters of Laertes, Ophelia and Polonius, who provide much of the secondary plot material in *Hamlet*. Like several scenes strategically placed throughout the play, Act I, scene iii is deliberately low-key, neither arousing strong emotions nor building dramatic tension. By this point in his career, Shakespeare was totally in command of dramatic rhythm. Act I, scene iii advances the plot and, in particular, supplies important information about Hamlet's relation to Ophelia, but its emotional level is calculated to relax the audience after the extraordinary impact of the first two scenes of *Hamlet*. Having allowed the audience to calm down, Shakespeare can now raise the emotional pitch of his play to new heights in the last two scenes of Act I. The second appearance of the ghost is even more impressive than the first and the fact that it has refused to speak for so long means that when it finally begins to talk, the audience, like Hamlet, hangs on its every word.

With the ghost's revelation of Claudius's crime, we are furnished with the last piece of information necessary to set the plot of *Hamlet* in motion.

In a traditional five-act structure, the second act develops the conflict established in the first. Shakespeare heightens the dramatic tension by creating both a plot and a counterplot in Act II of *Hamlet*. The act begins with a brief scene which develops the Polonius–Laertes subplot and allows the audience to calm down after the excitement generated by the end of Act I. By instructing his servant Reynaldo to spy on Laertes in Paris, Polonius introduces what is to be the major motif of Act II: one character trying to pry a secret out of another. When Ophelia enters with news of Hamlet's seemingly mad behaviour in her presence, Shakespeare creates the second mystery of his play. In Act II Hamlet begins his quest to validate the ghost's revelation: he feels a need to confirm by some independent means that Claudius did indeed kill his father. In order to conceal his purposes from Claudius, Hamlet puts on his antic disposition. But his odd behaviour arouses the king's suspicions and thus instigates the counterplot in Act II. While Hamlet is trying to search out Claudius's secret, Claudius feels compelled to search out Hamlet's.

Thus Act II initiates the metaphorical fencing match between Hamlet and Claudius. Protagonist and antagonist probe at each other, feinting, parrying, trying to thrust home into the depths of each other's souls. Each enlists aid in his quest to find out the truth about the other. Claudius employs first Polonius and then Rosencrantz and Guildenstern to interrogate Hamlet in Act II, scene ii, but the prince learns more from these encounters than his questioners do. And in the course of this scene, he acquires what are to be his principal allies in his plot against Claudius, the troupe of players which arrives in Denmark. Act II, scene ii is thus a remarkable exercise in dramatic economy: the action and dialogue advance at one and the same time Hamlet's plot against Claudius and Claudius's counterplot against Hamlet.

The introduction of the players adds another dimension to

Hamlet, what is often called a metadramatic dimension, an element of self-conscious theatricality. In a play in which all the characters on stage are of course actors, Shakespeare brings out a group of characters who are designated as actors by profession. They discuss their craft with Hamlet, reveal some of the tricks of their trade, give displays of their talent, and eventually even stage a play-within-the-play. At first sight, Shakespeare would appear to be running a risk by having all this theatrical activity take place on stage. He seems to be calling attention to the theatrical illusion, thereby working to undermine it. For example, one of the conventions theatre-goers in Shakespeare's day had to accept was the fact that all female roles were played by boys or young men. One would suppose that Elizabethan playwrights would not want their audiences to think about this potentially awkward situation, and yet Shakespeare has Hamlet joke about the male actors who must play female roles in the visiting company (II.ii.424–8), thus threatening to expose the theatrical practice as ridiculous.

But instead of destroying our sense of the reality of the play, the various player scenes complicate, deepen and enrich it. Drawing upon earlier dramatic experiments in plays such as *A Midsummer Night's Dream* (1595), Shakespeare by the time of writing *Hamlet* had learned how to use his theatrical medium itself as a source of dramatic images. The ghost's revelation has made Hamlet acutely aware of the gap between reality and illusion, and this recognition takes the form of his insight into Claudius's power as an actor: 'That one may smile, and smile, and be a villain!' (I.v.108). Thus Hamlet's epistemological concerns as a revenger naturally link up with his interest in the players and their capacity for creating illusions. Culminating in his soliloquy at the end of Act II, Hamlet is able to find an image of his own condition in the players he has seen perform. In the end, rather than reminding us that the reality of the action on stage is mere acting, the presence of the players in *Hamlet* suggests how much of what passes for action in the real world is in fact a form of acting. One reason why Shakespeare succeeds in making the metadramatic elements in *Hamlet* effective is that he integrates them into the play. The appearance of the players is not a mere digression from the main plot. Rather, Hamlet quickly thinks how to use them to advance his plot against Claudius. The players provide the prince with his most powerful weapon in his struggle with his uncle – the Mousetrap, the play that will 'catch the conscience of the King' (II.ii.605).

Hamlet's plan leads us directly into Act III, which in a traditional five-act structure contains the crisis or turning point of the play. Shakespeare handles the staging of *The Murder of Gonzago* with consummate skill. As many critics have observed, he shapes a poetic idiom for the play-within-the-play sufficiently artificial for it to stand out within the verse texture of *Hamlet*. Hamlet's commentary during the performance of the play adds a note of grotesque humour to the scene, as well as bitter irony. Moreover, the staging of the play-within-the-play is the culmination of the metadrama in *Hamlet*, as we the audience of the play soon find ourselves watching an audience within the play watching a play.

For all its subtlety, Act III, scene ii is also a brilliantly contrived bit of theatre, calculated to keep any audience on the edge of their seats. The genius of the scene lies in the way Shakespeare is able to focus attention on several points of interest at once. We are of course absorbed in *The Murder of Gonzago* itself, intent on seeing how Hamlet has set his trap for the king. But at the same time our eyes keep checking Claudius, waiting anxiously for the moment when the play will finally provoke a response from him. But we also have to keep an eye on Hamlet, because we want to know how he will react to Claudius's reaction. And finally our eyes are tempted to move all over the stage, for we also want to know how the court as a whole will react to Claudius's behaviour. By the time he finally rises and cries out 'Give me some light', the tension in the scene has become almost as unbearable for us as audience as it has for the king. In its use of a multiplicity of perspectives, and in particular of the principle of the audience voyeuristically spying on someone spying, Act III, scene ii of *Hamlet* generates as much suspense as the best work of the masters of motion picture thrillers, such as Fritz Lang and Alfred Hitchcock.

In the dramatic economy of *Hamlet*, Act III, scene ii supplies the turning point for both the plot and the counterplot, since it solves the mystery of Hamlet for Claudius even as it solves the mystery of Claudius for Hamlet. The prince finally believes that he knows for certain that his uncle killed his father and henceforth his course is clear: he must kill the king. But by the same token, Claudius now knows that Hamlet knows he killed his father, and hence the king's course is equally clear: he must have the prince killed. With a single element in the plot — the staging of the play-within-the-play — Shakespeare brings both Hamlet and Claudius to the point of no return in their enmity, and henceforth it may be expressed openly.

In the next scene, Shakespeare contrives an encounter between Claudius and Hamlet, which would seem to offer an opportunity for the prince to kill the king. But since he wishes to damn Claudius's soul as well as kill his body, Hamlet forgoes his first clear chance for revenge. We have already discussed the thematic importance of Act III, scene iii, which is central to our understanding of the impact of Hamlet's Christianity on his task as an avenger. We are now in a position to see the importance of the scene in the structure of the play. Perhaps the most distinctive characteristic of a traditional five-act structure is the fact that the crisis does not immediately lead to the catastrophe; that is, even though the turning point has been reached, the plot does not head straight for a resolution. The logic behind this structure is to maintain a balance or proportion between the first and second parts of the play, and to avoid making the resolution seem too easy. Thus in a traditional five-act structure, the rising action of Acts I and II is balanced by the falling action of Acts IV and V, and often fresh complications are introduced to delay the resolution. In Act III, scene iii Shakespeare appears to be playing with the possibilities of dramatic structure. He dangles before us the prospect of a swift and immediate conclusion to the play as Hamlet seriously contemplates killing Claudius. Part of us wants the play to end right here, but part of us wants it to continue, for we sense that much remains to be worked out in the fates of the characters, and the end of Claudius at this point would probably spell the end of Hamlet as well. Moreover, we share with the prince a sense that killing the king in Act III, scene iii would be too easy. Thus in dramatic terms, Act III, scene iii works to validate the logic of a traditional five-act structure: faced with the possibility of a swift conclusion, we in effect give our assent to a fourth and fifth act in the play.

In the accepted division of the play, Act III ends with the scene between Hamlet and Gertrude, in which he further seals his fate by inadvertently killing Polonius, thereby giving Claudius an excuse for shipping him out of the country. After the great public scene of Act III, scene ii, Shakespeare creates a contrast by shifting to this intimate dialogue between mother and son. But in its own way, Act III, scene iv is as intensely dramatic as Act III, scene ii, as Hamlet struggles to effect a change in his mother's heart. To emphasise the initial hostility between mother and son, Shakespeare resorts to a device he had used effectively in *Richard III*, the sharp, pointed, one-line, balanced, back-and-forth exchanges known in Greek drama as stichomythia:

Queen   Hamlet, thou hast thy father much offended.
Hamlet Mother, you have my father much offended.
Queen   Come, come you answer with an idle tongue.
Hamlet Go, go, you question with a wicked tongue.

(III.iv.9–12)

Hamlet's manic behaviour in this scene causes it to build in dramatic intensity, as first he seems to threaten violence against his mother and then actually commits it against Polonius. The way he obsessively dwells upon the sexual details of his mother's life raises the disturbing possibility that Hamlet may be losing control, and the reappearance of the ghost brings the scene to its peak of emotional excitement. In some ways, Hamlet is at his ugliest in this scene, in the way he speaks daggers to his mother and even more so in the way he uses daggers with Polonius (not to mention the callousness with which he says farewell to the old man's corpse). But Act III, scene iv is constructed like a little drama in itself, and it

builds up to a recognition and a reversal which show both
Gertrude and Hamlet at their best:

Queen   O Hamlet, thou hast cleft my heart in twain.
Hamlet O, throw away the worser part of it,
          And live the purer with the other half.   (III.iv.156–8)

The reconciliation which Hamlet brings about between
himself and his mother is one of the most moving moments
in the play, and indeed makes Act III, scene iv one of the
most affecting scenes Shakespeare ever wrote.

We turn now to Act IV, which is usually the main source
of difficulties in a traditional five-act structure. Because of
the required gap between the crisis and the catastrophe, a lull
in the action becomes inevitable, threatening to cause a let-
down for the audience. Dramatic excitement is at its peak at
the crisis and will build again as the catastrophe approaches,
but what is the playwright to do to keep the audience
occupied during the interim? In *Hamlet* Shakespeare came up
with an effective solution to the fourth-act problem. He
shifts attention to his secondary plot material, dealing with
what happens to Ophelia and Laertes. Hamlet is allowed
momentarily to recede into the background (from IV.iv to
V.i, he disappears from the stage − a gap of some 500 lines).
What happens to Ophelia and Laertes of course bears on the
fate of Hamlet, and Act IV does advance the action and
prepare for Act V. But for several scenes Shakespeare finds
a way of avoiding dealing with Hamlet directly, and he
develops the story of Ophelia and Laertes largely for its
intrinsic interest.

Indeed Act IV might be called Ophelia's act; though her
appearances are brief, she does become the emotional centre
of interest. The poignancy of her madness is perfectly con-
veyed by the songs she sings, which in their natural simplicity
and folk-song quality reflect her innocence (an innocence so
pure that it is unsullied and indeed set off by the off-colour
and bawdy passages in the songs). Her reappearances in the
act, and the pity she arouses, serve to counterpoint the tense
moments when Claudius manages to divert Laertes's anger

from himself to Hamlet. The brief scene when Ophelia distributes flowers to the assembled company on stage is beyond analysis: this is the kind of seemingly irrelevant, pointedly symbolic stage moment which only Shakespeare succeeds in fully integrating into a drama. The act ends with Gertrude's beautiful speech recounting Ophelia's death, a lyric moment when Shakespeare is able to suspend the action and give free rein to his poetic talent for word painting. Thus, if the dramatic intensity of Act IV threatens to flag after the high points of Act III, Shakespeare is able to compensate with the pathos of the scenes involving Ophelia, which grip the audience in a different way.

This is not to say that Shakespeare's focus on Ophelia causes him to lose sight of his play as a whole. In terms of contributing to the plot, Ophelia's death does provide the occasion for the confrontation between Hamlet and Laertes, and in thematic terms, Ophelia's authentic madness provides a revealing contrast to Hamlet's feigned madness. She is caught in a tragic bind resembling Hamlet's — divided between her love for her father and her love for the prince. But unlike Hamlet, Ophelia has no possible outlet for her troubled feelings in heroic action or indeed in any action of any kind. As a woman, she is condemned in her world to a purely passive role, and eventually her mind snaps under the strain of her inability to express her emotions. As we have seen, the Laertes of Act IV serves a similar thematic function as a foil to Hamlet, with his straightforwardness and singlemindedness as an avenger highlighting the complexity of Hamlet's response. But once again Shakespeare's thematic and dramatic purposes converge: because Laertes's situation as a son who has lost his father parallels Hamlet's, his story has an inherent dramatic interest as well. The moment in Act IV, scene iv when he breaks in at the head of a mob, threatening to overthrow Claudius, is very effective on stage. Moreover it provides an occasion for Claudius to reassert his stature, displaying courage in the way he stands up to Laertes and cunning in the way he manipulates his emotions against Hamlet. By having Claudius win Laertes over as an ally,

Shakespeare introduces the new complication which will stand in the way of Hamlet accomplishing his revenge.

With his protagonist and antagonist headed for a fatal collision in Act V, Shakespeare still finds ways to delay the expected catastrophe of a traditional five-act structure while maintaining the audience's interest. He saves one of his most brilliant theatrical strokes for the opening of Act V. The act is to be dominated by the idea of death, beginning with the funeral of Ophelia and culminating in the bloodbath that kills off the remaining principal characters. Shakespeare appropriately begins the act in a graveyard, but the way Act V opens violates all our expectations and our conventional sense of decorum. In the kind of scene which infuriated his neoclassical critics, especially in France, Shakespeare brings out a pair of rustic gravediggers, who, joking and punning about death, display a total disregard for the solemnity of the moment. When Hamlet enters, he engages one of the gravediggers in some of the most amusing dialogue of the play. In his *An Apology for Poetry* (1595), Sir Philip Sidney had censored this kind of 'mingling of kings and clowns', 'hornpipes and funerals' in early Elizabethan drama. But unlike his predecessors, Shakespeare knew what he was doing: the graveyard scene is the culmination of a strain of grotesque and macabre humour that runs throughout *Hamlet* and in many ways gives the play its distinctive flavour and colouration, the complexity of mood that lifts it above the common run of revenge plays.

Moreover, the gravediggers add a different perspective on death to the end of the play: for them, it is not an exceptional tragic moment but a part of their everyday lives (V.i.65–8). Paradoxically deriving their living from death, the gravediggers tend to accept it as part of the natural order. Their occupation puts them in touch with the perspective of eternity, from which individual deaths tend to pale into insignificance (V.i.41–59). Finally, as common men, the gravediggers remind us that there is a world beyond the tragic realm in which the noble characters of the play have become locked. Largely unaffected by and indifferent to the grand political happenings of *Hamlet*, the gravediggers have their doubts about the behaviour of 'great folk' (V.i.27). With death as the great leveller, their profession naturally leads them to question conventional distinctions of rank (V.i.29–33), and they end up provoking Hamlet's most skeptical comments about nobility and greatness (V.i.197–217). In sum, the graveyard scene is an example of Shakespeare's dramaturgy at its most daring. Precisely when he seems to come up with something inappropriate, the scene turns out to be profoundly appropriate on some deeper level. Though his play is properly headed towards its tragic conclusion, Shakespeare chooses to remind us just before the end that there are perspectives on life other than the tragic.

After Hamlet's run-in with Laertes at Ophelia's funeral, the stage is set for their final encounter, but Shakespeare provides one last opportunity for the audience to calm down before proceeding to the catastrophe. The last scene begins with Hamlet quietly conversing with Horatio, providing him – and us – with the details of what happened to the prince en route to England. The scene moves on to some comic byplay between Hamlet and the foppish courtier, Osric, as they discuss the terms of the impending fencing match with Laertes, though because we are aware of Claudius's plans, a serious undercurrent runs throughout this exchange. Finally we come to the combat itself, a grand scene staged before the entire court with great ceremony and an almost ritualistic quality, which links it with Act I, scene ii at the beginning of the play and Act III, scene ii in the middle. The duel naturally grips the audience's attention, especially given our knowledge of how Claudius and Laertes have rigged the contest. With Laertes and Hamlet run through by the poisoned blade, Gertrude poisoned by the drink, and Claudius poisoned by both the blade and the drink, *Hamlet* ends up with more violence on stage than any one of Shakespeare's other major tragedies. This conclusion is a good reminder that although critics have generally been fascinated by the inaction in *Hamlet*, the play actually contains enough action on stage to satisfy even the most vulgar and bloodthirsty audience. *Hamlet* is perhaps the

greatest tribute to Shakespeare's ability to create work of
intellectual and artistic substance which can nevertheless
please the widest possible audience.

The language of *Hamlet*

One aspect of Shakespeare's achievement in *Hamlet* remains
to be considered: his use of language. The play has become
as famous for its poetry as for its drama. But generally speaking Shakespeare subordinates the poetry to the drama, that is,
he shapes the poetry to serve his dramatic purposes.
Shakespeare's genius manifests itself in his ability to create
individual idioms for most of the major characters in the
play, and some of the minor ones as well. There are few plays
in which we hear so many distinct voices speak as we do in
Hamlet. For example, one of the challenges Shakespeare set
himself, and successfully met, was to differentiate the courtly
language of several of his characters. Shakespeare was aware
that elevated and even inflated diction is characteristic of
courtly speakers, but he was also aware that there are degrees
of elevation and inflation. Consider first Claudius's opening
lines:

> Though yet of Hamlet our dear brother's death
> The memory be green, and that it us befitted
> To bear our hearts in grief and our whole kingdom
> To be contracted in one brow of woe,
> Yet so far hath discretion fought with nature
> That we with wisest sorrow think on him
> Together with remembrance of ourselves.   (I.ii.1–7)

With its elaborate syntax and tendency toward circumlocu-
tion, this speech is clearly in the high style of the court.
Claudius could obviously express his thoughts in a simpler
and more direct fashion, but his aim is to impress the court
with his newly acquired dignity as a monarch: hence the insistent royal *we* ('our dear brother's death', 'us befitted', 'our
whole kingdom', 'we with wisest sorrow', 'remembrance of
ourselves'). Though the speech borders on pomposity with its
repetitiveness ('To bear our hearts with grief' and 'our whole

kingdom / To be contracted in one brow of woe' are after all the same idea), it stops short of outright bombast. Given our knowledge of Claudius's duplicity, we might wish to detect a false note in his speech, but in fact part of Shakespeare's initial effort to show Claudius in command as king is to show him in command of the language of a king. Though his speech is somewhat stilted and artificial, it is no more so than that of legitimate monarchs in Shakespeare, such as Henry V or Lear.

Now consider a speech to the court by Polonius:

> My liege, and madam, to expostulate
> What majesty should be, what duty is,
> Why day is day, night night, and time is time,
> Were nothing but to waste night, day, and time;
> Therefore, since brevity is the soul of wit,
> And tediousness the limbs and outward flourishes,
> I will be brief. Your noble son is mad:
> Mad call I it, for to define true madness,
> What is't but to be nothing else but mad?
> But let that go.   (II.ii.86–95)

At first sight, this speech might appear to be in Claudius's courtly idiom, with the same periodic sentences and the same kind of repetitions. But closer inspection reveals that Polonius oversteps the bounds within which Claudius just barely remains. Polonius repeats himself too often and too quickly ('why day is day, night night, and time is time'), and the artful rhetorical devices in his speech are too insistent. In his attempt to define madness, the stylistic principle of artful variation collapses into tautology. His speech is clearly a performance and he takes obvious pleasure in his own verbal skill. By calling attention to his linguistic tricks ('But let that go'), he makes his listeners concentrate, not on what he is saying, but on how he is saying it. (This speech provokes even Gertrude into a negative comment: 'More matter with less art', II.ii.95.) In short, Shakespeare skillfully manages to differentiate the strained but still basically dignified idiom of Claudius from the forced and bombastic idiom of Polonius, which contributes to our impression of him as a ludicrous old man.

Consider a third brand of courtly speech in *Hamlet*, Osric's attempt to describe Laertes to the prince:

Sir, here is newly come to court Laertes, believe me an absolute gentleman, full of most excellent differences, of very soft society, and great showing; indeed, to speak sellingly of him, he is the card or calendar of gentry: for you shall find in him the continent of what part a gentleman would see.   (V.ii.106–11)

Like the other courtiers, Osric attempts to elevate and inflate his diction, essentially saying the same thing over and over again — that Laertes is a gentleman — but doing so in one fashionable phrase after another ('the card or calendar of gentry'). The first thing to remark about this speech is that it is in prose, and appropriately so, since Osric is not addressing the assembled court, as Claudius and Polonius were in the above examples. Osric is having a private conversation with Hamlet and thus could afford to relax his speech. But what Shakespeare shows is that for Osric, the idiom of courtly speech carries over even into his intimate conversations. Osric is such a creature of the court that, wherever he goes, he remains a captive of its inflated idiom and above all its inability to call things by their ordinary names. In Osric we see what happens when the rhetoric of the court filters down to its underlings: language begins to lose touch with any reality except what is currently fashionable in the court.

Osric's overelaborate speech provokes a scornful reply from Hamlet:

Sir, his definement suffers no perdition in you, though I know to divide him inventorially would dozy th' arithmetic of memory, and yet but yaw neither in respect of his quick sail; but in the verity of extolment, I take him to be a soul of great article, and his infusion of such dearth and rareness as, to make true diction of him, his semblable is his mirror, and who else would trace him, his umbrage, nothing more.   (V.ii.112–20)

Hamlet here carries the courtly inflation of diction to new extremes, pouring fourth a cascade of fancy words ('definement', 'perdition', 'inventorially', 'verity of extolment'). By the time Hamlet is through, the courtly idiom has been elevated to the point of unintelligibility. Like Polonius, Hamlet overuses the standard devices of courtly rhetoric, but the dramatic context still allows us to discriminate between their voices. Because Polonius speaks the way he does on his own initiative, his language comes across as unconscious self-parody. Because Hamlet by contrast is provoked into his mode of speech and is clearly responding to Osric, his speech strikes us as intentional parody, a clever expression of his contempt for the court.

Thus, even within the seemingly uniform category of courtly speech, Shakespeare creates a whole spectrum of courtly idiom, running from the relatively kingly speech of Claudius, through the almost senile pompousness of Polonius, to the servile mimicry of Osric, even including Hamlet's bitter parody of courtly style. Compared to the famous soliloquies of Hamlet, the speeches I have discussed may seem like minor elements in the play. But the point is that Shakespeare shows his genius in the minor details of *Hamlet* as well. The man who could write 'To be, or not to be,' could also create the distinctive idiom of Osric, and both achievements contribute to the success of *Hamlet* as a whole. To be sure, we put a higher premium on the speech of Hamlet, and it is difficult to escape the impression that Shakespeare gave more of his own verbal talent to Hamlet than he did to any other character he ever created. Certainly, whereas the other characters in the play tend to sound one characteristic note, Hamlet ranges up and down the entire scale, from the barbed humour of his exchanges with Polonius to the imaginative heights of his speculations about the afterlife. The extraordinary range of Hamlet's idiom is sometimes evident within a single speech, as examination of any one of his soliloquies will show.

His third soliloquy, for example – 'O, what a rogue and peasant slave am I!' (II.ii.550) – illustrates how swiftly Hamlet can change his mood as well as his language. He begins by reflecting in a syntactically complex question on the paradox of an actor's ability to display real emotion in a fictional situation (II.ii.551–7). His thoughts crystallise in two lines which in their balance and pointed quality have the perfection of a classical epigram:

> What's Hecuba to him, or he to Hecuba,
> That he should weep for her?   (II.ii.559–60)

As Hamlet turns to apply the lesson of the actor to his own case, his speech becomes increasingly frantic. The soliloquy reaches its peak of excitement in a moment of intense self-questioning and self-dramatisation, when Hamlet imagines himself interacting with an antagonist:

>   Am I a coward?
> Who calls me villain, breaks my pate across,
> Plucks off my beard and blows it in my face,
> Tweaks me by the nose, gives me the lie i' th' throat
> As deep as to the lungs?   (II.ii.571–5)

We have come a long way in a short time: from the sublime poignancy of Hamlet's meditation on the meaning of Hecuba to the image of the Prince of Denmark being tweaked by the nose. Shakespeare does not restrict Hamlet to the elevated courtly diction decorum would normally dictate for a prince. Indeed, just a few lines later, Hamlet resorts to the most vulgar language, calling himself 'pigeon-liver'd' and 'an ass' (II.ii.577, 582), and comparing himself to a 'whore' and 'a very drab / A stallion' (II.ii.585–7; 'scullion' in the Folio reading). This movement is an example of what Erich Auerbach characterised in his *Mimesis* as the mixed style in Shakespeare: 'the element of physical creaturalness, that of lowly everyday objects, and that of the mixture of classes involving persons of high rank and low rank' (313). Auerbach viewed this style as particularly characteristic of Hamlet's speech: 'He jumps from the obscene to the lyrical or sublime, from the ironically incongruous to dark and profound meditation' (316).

This mixture of style can even be found in some of Hamlet's sustained passages in prose, for example, this speech to Rosencrantz and Guildenstern:

I will tell you why, so shall my anticipation prevent your discovery, and your secrecy to the King and Queen moult no feather. I have of late − but wherefore I know not − lost all my mirth, forgone all custom of exercises; and indeed it goes so heavily with my disposition, that this goodly frame, the earth, seems to me a sterile promontory; this most excellent canopy, the air, look you, this brave o'erhanging firmament, this majestical roof fretted with golden fire, why, it appeareth nothing to me but a foul and pestilent congregation of vapors. What a piece of work is a man, how noble in reason, how infinite in faculties, in form and moving, how express and admirable in action, how like an angel in apprehension, how like a god! the beauty of the world; the paragon of animals; and yet to me what is this quintessence of dust? Man delights not me – nor women neither, though by your smiling you seem to say so.

(II.ii.292–310)

This speech arises naturally out of Hamlet's dialogue with Rosencrantz and Guildenstern as he discovers that they have appeared in Elsinore at the request of the king and queen. The quaint, almost barnyard imagery of his opening sentence ('moult no feather') seems to promise a colloquial speech, and the way Hamlet begins to open up his heart to his old friends further suggests that the speech will remain on the conversational level. But Hamlet's speech quickly modulates into something higher, as his agile mind begins to move outward from his immediate situation to adopt a worldwide and then a cosmic perspective. Though the speech remains in prose, it soon develops something like the rhythms of poetry, with the neat balance of its antithetical clauses. Consider, for example, how 'this majestical roof fretted with golden fire' is counterpointed against 'a foul and pestilent congregation of vapors' to convey a sense of the tension of extremes within Hamlet's mind. Similarly, Hamlet's vision of man is built up in one parallel clause after another, only to be punctured by the one pointed phrase, 'quintessence of dust'. Just when Hamlet appears to be breaking out of the dramatic frame into some kind of set speech, he notices how his listeners are reacting and brings himself back down to earth. His speech ends as it began in the conversational mode, with Hamlet making a joke for the benefit of his schoolfellows.

In the way it ranges from moulting feathers to 'this goodly frame, the earth', this speech reveals in microcosm the extraordinary scope of Hamlet's idiom, as well as of the mind it reflects, while also showing the agility with which he moves back and forth between the poles of the serious and the comic.

It is also a good reminder that Shakespeare is not simply the greatest poet in the English language; he is the greatest master of prose as well. But as tempted as one may be to excerpt such a magnificent passage and dwell upon the beauty of its language, one must not forget how well Shakespeare weaves it into the fabric of the dialogue. Shakespeare had impressive resources as a shaper of language, but what is even more impressive is the way he placed those resources in the service of his dramatic vision.

Chapter 4

The heritage of *Hamlet*

Hamlet in the seventeenth and eighteenth centuries

We do not have any contemporary reviews of the first performances of *Hamlet* or records of box office receipts. But
what evidence we do have suggests that the play captivated
audiences from the start. At least Shakespeare's fellow
playwrights thought so: the way they began almost immediately imitating *Hamlet* suggests that they were trying to
capitalise on the success of an unusually popular play.
Donald Joseph McGinn has devoted a book of over 200 pages
just to tracing the influence of *Hamlet* on plays written between 1600 and 1642. McGinn catalogues hundreds of allu-
sions to *Hamlet*, as well as many imitations of individual
characters and scenes from the play. *Eastward Hoe!* (1605),
a collaborative effort by John Marston, George Chapman
and Ben Jonson, even contains a character named Hamlet.
He is a footman, and when he rushes in asking for his lady's
coach, he is greeted with the words: 'Sfoot! Hamlet, are you
mad?' (III.ii.6). The fact that other dramatists could rely on
their audience's familiarity with *Hamlet* to make such jokes
work is one index of the initial popularity of the play.

When the Puritans forced the closing of the London
theatres in 1642, they interrupted the stage history of *Hamlet*,
but they could not keep the play off the boards for more than
a few years. With the Restoration, the London theatres were
reopened in 1660, and it did not take long for someone to
decide to revive *Hamlet*. Sir William D'Avenant staged it at
his new theatre in Lincoln's Inn Fields in the summer of
1661. Though the play was adapted to suit the tastes of
Restoration audiences, it was not mutilated almost beyond
recognition, as happened to many of Shakespeare's other
plays. (Nahum Tate, for example, gave *King Lear* a happy

ending, in which Lear survives and Cordelia marries Edgar.)
D'Avenant basically left the structure of *Hamlet* intact, while
substantially cutting the text. He dropped nearly all the Fortinbras material, eliminated the characters of Voltemand
and Cornelius, and omitted Polonius's advice to Laertes,
Hamlet's advice to the players, and his soliloquy 'O what a
rogue and peasant slave am I'.

What we find most objectionable today in D'Avenant's
version is his feeble attempt to refine and improve
Shakespeare's diction. At times he was merely trying to
remove impious expressions from the play, especially oaths.
At other times, he seems to have been trying to make the
verse more regular and to clear up obscurities in the text.
D'Avenant's alterations in the wording of the 'To be, or not
to be' soliloquy seem particularly pointless and ill-conceived.
He changed 'the native hue of resolution' to 'the healthful
face of resolution' and Shakespeare's powerful line, 'Is
sicklied o'er with the pale cast of thought', became the much
weaker 'Shews sick and pale with thought' (III.i.83–4).

In general, adaptations of *Hamlet* like D'Avenant's can
teach us much about the power of Shakespeare's play. On the
one hand, attempts to improve on Shakespeare inevitably
backfire and reveal the shortcomings of the adapter. The
wisdom of Shakespeare's original decisions about the
language and plot of the play becomes clearer when someone
tries other possibilities. On the other hand, as the success of
D'Avenant's version shows, *Hamlet* is powerful enough as
theatre to withstand misguided efforts to improve upon the
play. The genius of Shakespeare's original conception shines
through, even beneath the prettified surface D'Avenant tried
to spread over the play.

In various versions and adaptations, *Hamlet* continued to
please audiences throughout the eighteenth century. Any
actor who aspired to pre-eminence in the theatre eventually
had to undertake the role, and many established their reputations on the basis of their success as the Prince of Denmark.
In the second half of the eighteenth century, David Garrick
was particularly admired for his interpretation of Hamlet.

But perhaps more importantly, it was in the eighteenth century that *Hamlet* began to extend its influence beyond the borders of the stage. Critics began to puzzle over *Hamlet*, especially the question of the hero's delay. Once *Hamlet* was viewed as literature, that is, as a great work of poetry which requires careful reading and analysis, critics began asking questions about the play which might well escape the casual viewer in the theatre.

Hamlet in the nineteenth century

The Romantics discovered hitherto unplumbed depths in *Hamlet*, partly by projecting their own concerns on to the play. For example, Coleridge's famous interpretation of Hamlet's delay as the product of too much thinking is obviously a case of his attributing his own mental indecisiveness to Shakespeare's character. But the Romantics did not simply remake Hamlet in their own image. Their new ideas and attitudes made them alert to aspects of the play which had escaped earlier generations. In particular, the Romantics focused on the longing for the infinite in Hamlet, his dissatisfaction with the finite boundaries of his existence and his fascination with what lies beyond the horizons of ordinary human life. As we have seen, this is in fact an aspect of Shakespeare's characterisation of Hamlet, and Romantic critics did well to call attention to it. What they did not see as clearly is that Shakespeare shows what is questionable in Hamlet's longing for the infinite and in that sense provides a kind of proleptic critique of Romanticism.

Perhaps the most important document of the new fascination with *Hamlet* is Goethe's *Wilhelm Meisters Lehrjahre* (*Wilhelm Meister's Apprenticeship*), originally published in 1795–6. Many people who refer to Goethe's theory of Hamlet are unaware that, strictly speaking, it is not Goethe's theory at all but rather that of one of his characters. It is in the course of a dialogue with his fellow actors that Wilhelm Meister speaks the passage that is so often cited as Goethe's own theory:

To me it is clear that Shakespeare meant . . . to represent the effects of a great action laid upon a soul unfit for the performance of it . . . There is an oak-tree planted in a costly jar, which should have borne only pleasant flowers in its bosom: the roots expand, the jar is shivered. A lovely, pure, noble, and most moral nature, without the strength of nerve which forms a hero, sinks beneath a burden it cannot bear and must not cast away.

(Book IV, Chapter 13, 234)

We have already seen the limitations of this view of Hamlet; it is unfortunate that this one passage is often taken for the sum total of Goethe's wisdom on the play. In fact, *Wilhelm Meister* is filled with interesting observations about *Hamlet*, including a penetrating analysis of the character of Ophelia (in particular, a perceptive defence of the bawdiness of her songs).

While in its treatment of the psychology of Shakespeare's characters *Wilhelm Meister* looks forward to modern interpretations of *Hamlet*, it also looks back to eighteenth-century attitudes towards the play, especially the urge to revise and improve it. Wilhelm is given the task of preparing a new text for a production of *Hamlet*, and tries to eliminate what he regards as Shakespeare's errors in the plot. Here is how Wilhelm decides to rework the political background to *Hamlet*:

After the death of Hamlet the father, the Norwegians, lately con-quered, grow unruly. The viceroy of that country sends his son, Horatio, an old school-friend of Hamlet's . . . to Denmark, to press forward the equipment of the fleet, which, under the new luxurious king, proceeds but slowly . . . The new sovereign gives Horatio audience, and sends Laertes into Norway with intelligence that the fleet will soon arrive; whilst Horatio is commissioned to accelerate the preparation of it: and the Queen, on the other hand, will not con-sent that Hamlet, as he wishes, should go to sea along with him.

(284; V, 4)

These may seem like minor and insignificant alterations, but this attempt to simplify the movements of the characters in *Hamlet* would in fact destroy the carefully planned symbolic geography of the play, and above all the contrast between the worlds north and south of Shakespeare's Denmark. But despite this regrettable impulse to tinker with the play, the way a writer of Goethe's stature responded to Shakespeare's genius in *Hamlet* is perhaps the best illustration of its status as genuine *world* literature.

Given the nineteenth century's interest in *Hamlet*, it was inevitable that someone would turn the play into an opera. That someone turned out to be the French composer, Ambroise Thomas. Thomas's *Hamlet* was first produced in 1868 at the Paris Opéra, where by all accounts it was a great success. The opera remained in the active Paris repertoire until 1938, receiving hundreds of performances. It is occasionally revived today as a historical curiosity, but a modern audience has many hurdles to overcome in an effort to appreciate Thomas's transformation of *Hamlet* – or even just to take it seriously. Ophélie's greatly expanded role is a good indication of what Thomas did to *Hamlet*, namely to reconceive it as a typical operatic love story. Much of the first act is devoted to a semi-rapturous love duet between Hamlet and Ophélie.

Thomas's reliance on operatic conventions leads him into one blunder after another in his *Hamlet*. One of his most bizarre additions is a long drinking song which constitutes the heart of Hamlet's interaction with the players in Thomas's version. Welcoming them to Denmark, the prince calls for wine and celebrates its enchanting power to bring balm and oblivion to his heart. One would think that Hamlet's open contempt for Claudius's drinking in Shakespeare's version would have suggested to Thomas or his librettists that praise of drunkenness would be out of character for the melancholy prince. But Thomas evidently could not resist the temptation to write the kind of drinking song (the so-called *brindisi*) which was a stock scene in nineteenth-century opera, the kind of scene which Verdi and Boito use so effectively in their *Otello* (1887). They knew enough, however, to give such a song, not to Otello, but to Iago, for whom praising the power of wine is in character and in fact an integral part of his plot against Cassio. By contrast, having Hamlet sing the praises of wine does nothing to advance the plot and suggests that Thomas either failed to understand his character or just had no interest in coming up with a consistent portrayal of the prince.

The ending of Thomas's *Hamlet* is the most controversial aspect of the opera. In the original version Thomas and his librettists provided a happy ending. Hamlet and Laërte forego their hostilities when they catch sight of Ophélie's funeral procession; then the ghost reappears to command Hamlet to kill Claudius and send Gertrude to a convent; finally the ghost proclaims Hamlet king. Even Thomas realised that this ending might strike some audiences as unsatisfactory; hence he wrote an alternate finale, in which Hamlet kills Claudius but then commits suicide. Given the composer's uncertainty about how to end his opera, performers have experimented with a variety of conclusions. When Dame Nellie Melba sang the role of Ophélie, for example, she had the opera simply end with her mad-scene. The fact that Thomas's *Hamlet* permits such tinkering and tampering with so important a part as the conclusion points to its lack of artistic integrity.

The comic *Hamlet*

Thomas's *Hamlet* seems at times to border on a travesty of Shakespeare's play, but we can be certain that the humour is unintentional. The nineteenth century was, however, the great era of intentional parodies and burlesques of *Hamlet*. Perhaps the increasing veneration in which the play was held began prompting writers to try to take it down a peg or two. The reworkings of *Hamlet* are conveniently collected in Stanley Wells's five-volume set, *Nineteenth-Century Shakespeare Burlesques*, which includes no fewer than ten versions. They almost all include songs, which transform familiar lines from *Hamlet* into 'something wondrous strange'. Here, for example, is how the opening lines of Hamlet's first soliloquy appear in John Poole's *Hamlet Travestie* (1810), sung to the tune of 'Derry Down':

> A ducat I'd give if a sure way I knew
> How to thaw and resolve my stout flesh into dew!

How happy were I if no sin was self-slaughter!
For I'd then throw myself and my cares in the water.

(I, 10–11)

In an American travesty, *Hamlet Revamped* (1874) by
Charles C. Soule, 'To be, or not to be' is sung to the tune of
'Three blind mice' (V, 208). As one might expect, the 'To be,
or not to be' speech is a particular favourite of the parodists,
appearing in such metamorphoses as 'to drink, or not to
drink!' (III, 90) or 'to pop, or not to pop the fatal question'
(IV, 314). Perhaps the most memorable version of the soliloquy occurs in the anonymous *Hamlet! The Ravin' Prince of
Denmark!! or, The Baltic Swell!!! and the Diving Belle!!!!*
(1866):

> 'To be or not to be, that is the question,'
> Oh dear! I'm suffering from the indigestion!
> 'Whether 'tis nobler in the mind to suffer
> The slings and arrows of' − a paltry duffer;
> 'Or to take arms, and by opposing end them' −
> These rhymes are very poor, I can't amend them −
> To sleep away the pain of too much grub;
> 'To sleep − perchance to dream − aye, there's the rub.'

(IV, 107)

Several of the *Hamlet* parodies use the opportunity to
modernise the story. For example, in A. C. Hilton's *Hamlet,
or Not Such a Fool as He Looks* (1882), the prince uses the
techniques of a modern seance to raise his father's ghost. The
most interesting modernisations involve the final combat between Hamlet and Laertes. In the anonymous *A Thin Slice of
Ham let!* (c. 1863), they meet in a shooting match. Poole
began a new stage tradition of having Hamlet and Laertes
enter a boxing ring to settle their differences. This tradition
reached its dubious culmination in *Hamlet! The Ravin'
Prince of Denmark!!*, in which all the techniques of modern
publicity are enlisted to heighten the drama of the final scene
and the Hamlet–Laertes confrontation is billed as 'King
Claudius' Big un v. the Danish Chicken' (IV, 131).

Though it may be difficult to believe, I have tried to select
the funnier moments from the versions of *Hamlet* Wells
reprints. Their humour, such as it is, is hardly subtle and they

contribute little or nothing to our understanding or enjoyment of Shakespeare's play. But Wells does include one work of lasting merit: *Rosencrantz and Guildenstern* (1874) by W. S. Gilbert, the Gilbert of Gilbert and Sullivan. Gilbert accepts the fact of being a latecomer to the *Hamlet* tradition and incorporates an awareness of the accumulation of speculation concerning the prince into the world of his play. His Ophelia finds Hamlet a mystery precisely because she must approach him through the mediation of theatrical tradition. When Guildenstern asks her what the prince is like, she expresses her bewilderment at the multiplicity of stage Hamlets:

> Alike for no two seasons at a time.
> Sometimes he's tall − sometimes he's very short −
> Now with black hair − now with a flaxen wig −
> Sometimes an English accent − then a French −
> Then English with a strong provincial 'burr.'   (IV, 249)

Gilbert creates humour through a self-conscious treatment of theatrical conventions. For example, in his play, Gertrude's greatest fear is not her son's madness, but something about his stage demeanour:

> *Rosencrantz*   How gloomily he stalks,
> As one o'erwhelmed with weight of anxious care.
> He thrusts his hand into his bosom − thus −
> Starts − looks around − then, as if reassured,
> Rumples his hair and rolls his glassy eyes!
> *Queen* (*Appalled*) − That means − he's going to soliloquize!
> Prevent this, gentlemen, by any means!   (IV, 251)

Instructed by their Queen, Rosencrantz and Guildenstern proceed to play games with Hamlet, violating the most basic convention of the soliloquy and completing Hamlet's half-formed thoughts:

> *Hamlet* To be − or not to be!
> *Rosencrantz*   Yes − that's the question −
>   (IV, 252)

In moments such as these, Gilbert makes our familiarity with *Hamlet* work for him, rather than against him (as tends to happen with the other *Hamlet* parodies).

Gilbert's *Rosencrantz and Guildenstern* forms a kind of

peak in the range of *Hamlet* parodies. But the tradition of parodying *Hamlet* has continued undiminished into this century, even in films and television, proving that the play is still sufficiently popular that any audience may be expected to recognise a reference to it. For example, no one would accuse the American television series *Gilligan's Island* (1964–7) of catering to a high-brow audience. And yet in one episode a Broadway producer with the apt name of Harold Hecuba (played by Phil Silvers) is temporarily marooned on the island with the castaways. For his benefit, they stage a musical version of *Hamlet*, complete with 'Neither a borrower nor a lender be' sung to the tune of the *Toreador* song from Bizet's *Carmen*. It is doubtful that the writers of this show (Gerald Gardner and Dee Caruso) realised that they were working within a long tradition of *Hamlet* parodies that stretches back into the nineteenth century, and yet the resemblance of their work to the plays Wells reprints is uncanny.

Hamlet in the twentieth century

It may seem odd to dwell at such length on comic versions of one of the world's great tragedies. But any full appreciation of the place of the play in our culture should acknowledge that it has not always been an object of reverence. And in a strange way, the comic versions of *Hamlet* in the nineteenth century, however crude they may be, point more clearly in the direction of twentieth-century treatments of *Hamlet* than all the efforts of Romantic and Victorian critics to view the play as a kind of sacred text. For what is most characteristic of twentieth-century reworkings of *Hamlet* is their ironic mode.

This does not mean that every twentieth-century author who has attempted to recreate the play has treated it ironically. In fact, versions of *Hamlet* have proliferated to such an extent in the modern period that it is impossible to categorise them simply or even to survey them in a brief chapter. Martin Scofield has written a whole book called *The Ghosts of Hamlet* which discusses the place of the play in modern literature, taking up such writers as Mallarmé, Claudel,

Valéry, Laforgue, T. S. Eliot, Joyce, D. H. Lawrence and Kafka. Given the extent of *Hamlet* literature in the twentieth century, I have chosen to concentrate on what strikes me as new and distinctive in modern approaches to the play: the effort to do with serious intent what the nineteenth-century parodists were doing for comic effect, namely to cut the play down to size. The twentieth century is very much the heir of the nineteenth century's veneration of *Hamlet*, but has reacted against it. Having emerged as a cultural icon, the play has become subject to the iconoclastic tendencies of modernism. One way of establishing one's independence from artistic tradition has been to show that one is no longer under the spell of *Hamlet*.

A work which was prophetic of the way the twentieth century has treated *Hamlet* was appropriately written in 1899 by the Greek poet, C. P. Cavafy. Long before critics like G. Wilson Knight began defending Claudius and blaming Hamlet for all the troubles in Denmark, Cavafy chose to take the side of the king against the prince. In his poem 'King Claudius', Cavafy presents Hamlet's antagonist as a decent and humane ruler:

> He was quiet
> and meek; and he loved peace
> (the land had suffered much
> from the battles of his predecessor).
> He acted courteously to everyone
> great and small. He hated high-handed
> acts, and he always sought
> counsel on the affairs of state from
> serious-minded and experienced people. (252)

Trying to give the impression of impartiality, Cavafy goes on to explain how Hamlet could ever have wanted to kill such a good king, but in the process he only succeeds in making the prince look even worse:

> Just why his nephew killed him
> they never stated with certainty.
> He suspected him of murder.
> The basis of his suspicion was
> that one night as he was walking

on one of the ancient bastions
he thought he saw a ghost
and he made conversation with the ghost.
And presumably he learned from the ghost
some accusation against the king.

It is remarkable how in such a brief poem — in the English translation the whole consists of only 91 lines — Cavafy is able to make us take a fresh look at Shakespeare's *Hamlet*. Stated this baldly, Hamlet's case against Claudius begins to dissolve before our eyes, and we suddenly want to put the prince on trial. Indeed we have to force ourselves to remember that Shakespeare gives us objective evidence for Claudius's guilt, not just Hamlet's vague, subjective impressions.

Why would Cavafy write such a poem? It is not likely that he had any interest in rewriting Danish history or that he had any real concern for Claudius's reputation. What makes 'King Claudius' a modernist poem is that it is an exercise in perspectivism. Cavafy demonstrates that with a simple change in our point of view, all the events in a work we thought we knew well suddenly can look completely different and perhaps take on a new meaning. Viewing *Hamlet* from something other than the usual perspective we share with the prince teaches us something about the relativity of all perspectives. There may even be something anti-heroic in Cavafy's poem: hence his preference for the peaceful Claudius over the warlike Hamlet family.

We may well feel that Cavafy is being unfair to Hamlet, and giving a one-sided view of his character. But fairness to Hamlet is not the aim of Cavafy's poem. The prince only appears to be the object of the poet's skepticism in 'King Claudius'; his real target is Shakespeare himself. The elevation of Hamlet as a hero in our culture is really a measure of our elevation of Shakespeare himself into a cultural hero. The uneasiness with *Hamlet* many modern authors have displayed may thus reflect the phenomenon Harold Bloom has called the anxiety of influence. Faced with Shakespeare as the pre-eminent artist in the Western literary tradition, authors are constantly looking for ways to come to terms with his achievement and make room for their own creativity. This often involves a search for ways to cut the giant Shakespeare down to manageable size and one way to do so is to cut his heroes down to more ordinary human proportions. As a reading of *Hamlet*, Cavafy's 'King Claudius' is an example of what Bloom calls poetic misreading or misprision. By giving an antithetical view of Claudius, Cavafy tries to show the partiality of Shakespeare's portrait of Hamlet, and thus to demonstrate that even the immortal Shakespeare has his limitations.

Perspectivism has proved to be the key to twentieth-century reworkings of *Hamlet*. Writers have seized upon the notion that Shakespeare told only part of the story in *Hamlet* because he told it largely from the perspective of the prince. The great temptation for twentieth-century authors has been to retell the story to reduce its heroic dimensions; above all, they try to efface the distinction between Hamlet and the other characters by bringing out their perspective on events. John Barth enunciates the principle of this approach in his novel *The End of the Road* (1958), when a psychotherapist is explaining a new technique called mythotherapy to a potential patient:

In life there are no essentially major or minor characters. To that extent all fiction and biography, and most historiography, are a lie. Everyone is necessarily the hero of his own life story. *Hamlet* could be told from Polonius' point of view and called *The Tragedy of Polonius, Lord Chamberlain of Denmark*. He didn't think he was a minor character in anything, I daresay. (83)

In fact, Shakespeare's play works precisely to make clear to us the gulf which separates a Hamlet from a Polonius. Thus Barth's principle of 'every man a hero in his own story' runs directly counter to Shakespeare's notion of nobility, and hence works to call into question his distinctive stature as a playwright.

The author who worked most systematically to carry out Barth's proposal for rewriting *Hamlet* is Tom Stoppard. In his *Rosencrantz and Guildenstern Are Dead* (1967), *Hamlet* meets *Waiting for Godot*, and *Waiting for Godot* wins. That is, by rewriting *Hamlet* from the perspective of two of the most minor of characters, Stoppard manages to turn the play into Theatre of the Absurd. Given the limited comprehension Rosencrantz and Guildenstern have of what is going on around them, events in Denmark inevitably strike them as a meaningless sequence of pointless actions. Stoppard interweaves actual passages from the original *Hamlet* with the new dialogue he creates for Rosencrantz and Guildenstern. The result is a *tour de force*: lines which we are used to taking seriously suddenly appear ridiculous in the new context Stoppard creates for them. In particular, he understands how repetition and compression can reduce even the most powerful passages to triviality. Consider what happens to some of the most famous words of Shakespeare's Hamlet when Stoppard's Rosencrantz and Guildenstern repeat them as they review their questioning of the prince:

And what did we get in return? He's depressed! . . . Denmark's a prison and he'd rather live in a nutshell; some shadow-play about the nature of ambition, which never got down to cases, and finally one direct question, which might have led somewhere, and led in fact to his illuminating claim to tell a hawk from a handsaw.   (57)

Continuing his fascination with *Hamlet*, in 1979 Stoppard published a pair of Shakespeare adaptations, *Dogg's Hamlet, Cahoot's Macbeth*. A full examination of these two plays would require a discussion of how they complement each other, and even *Dogg's Hamlet* by itself – a Wittgensteinian experiment in language – is too complicated to explain in brief. But part of *Dogg's Hamlet* consists of what Stoppard refers to as *The Dogg's Troupe 15-Minute Hamlet*, 'which,' as he explains, 'was written (or rather edited) for performance on a double-decker bus' (7). The 15-minute *Hamlet* is exactly what its title suggests – a version of Shakespeare's *Hamlet* edited down so that it can be performed – admittedly at breakneck pace – within 15 minutes. When the play is over, as an encore the cast replays the entire story, this time in an even more drastically edited version, which passes by even more quickly.

The 15-minute *Hamlet* is another theatrical *tour de force*. Stoppard uses only authentic lines from *Hamlet* and he manages to convey the essentials of the action. But once again he succeeds in creating a Brechtian alienation effect. With all the omissions, familiar lines jar together in unfamiliar contexts, and our overall sense of *Hamlet* is unhinged. One can get a feeling for how the play proceeds from the prologue, spoken by the figure of Shakespeare as he accepts the applause of the audience:

> For this relief, much thanks.
> Though I am native here, and to the manner born,
> It is a custom more honoured in the breach
> Than in the observance.
> Well.
> Something is rotten in the state of Denmark.
> To be, or not to be, that is the question.
> There are more things in heaven and earth
> Then are dreamt of in your philosophy –
> There's a divinity that shapes our ends,
> Rough hew them how we will
> Though this be madness, yet there is method in it.
> I must be cruel only to be kind;
> Hold, as t'were, the mirror up to nature.
> A countenance more in sorrow than in anger.   (31–2)

This is the text of the *Hamlet* we know and admire, and it even has a kind of crazy logic to it, but when the lines rush by us at this speed and out of order, they are again reduced to absurdity. Indeed in the elaborate context Stoppard creates in *Dogg's Hamlet* for his 15-minute version, it is literally being performed in a language foreign to those who view it. Perhaps Stoppard is trying to suggest that through repetition *Hamlet* has lost its meaning for us, that we have become so familiar with the play that, whenever we stage it, we are just going through the motions and might as well get it over with as soon as possible.

Plays such as *Rosencrantz and Guildenstern Are Dead* and *Dogg's Hamlet* thus take their place in the ongoing process of each age reinterpreting Shakespeare's play. The Restoration had its Restoration *Hamlets*, the Romantics had their

Romantic *Hamlets*, and the twentieth century has found its absurdist *Hamlets*. Shakespeare's play is rich enough to offer a basis for each reinterpretation, revision, and reworking. Awakening to a new sense of the infinite possibilities of human nature, the Romantics found this sense prefigured in Hamlet. For them, Hamlet became a Romantic, a man faced with an overabundance of choices, refusing to commit himself to any determinate form of existence, a forerunner of Schiller's Wallenstein. By a similar process, twentieth-century authors have found intuitions of modern nihilism in Hamlet's view of the world. Once again they begin from something that is genuinely in Shakespeare's play. We have seen that Hamlet's view of the futility and meaninglessness of heroic action is an integral part of his character. But like the Romantics, the modern proponents of an absurdist *Hamlet* are seeing only one aspect of Shakespeare's play. They are too ready to identify Shakespeare's own view with Hamlet's, and fail to see the ways in which the playwright maintains a critical perspective on his hero. Just as Shakespeare shows what is problematic in Hamlet's longing for the infinite, he calls into question his sense of the futility of life as well. Indeed the two points are profoundly connected: Hamlet's nihilistic doubts about the the efficacy of heroic action are in fact the reverse side of his initial sense of the infinity of human potential. It is only the heights of Hamlet's original hopes for man that lead him into the depths of his despair. In a sense, then, the Romantic Hamlet of infinite possibility and the modern Hamlet of nihilistic despair are mirror images of each other.

One could virtually write a history of the past four centuries of European literature in terms of the reception of *Hamlet*. I thus have had to pass over many rewritings of the play which are as interesting as those I have chosen to discuss. For example, in 1977 the East German playwright Heiner Müller published a bizarre work entitled *Hamletmaschine* ('Hamletmachine'), which shows how the play has been enlisted in contemporary political struggles. Müller transforms Ophelia into a terrorist, modelled on Ulrike Meinhof, who concludes the play with a quotation from Squeaky Fromme (the former Manson family member who tried to assassinate President Ford). Indeed by the time Müller is through with *Hamlet*, it finally has been transformed almost beyond recognition, as the following stage directions suggest:

Out of an up-ended coffin, labelled HAMLET 1, step Claudius and Ophelia, the latter dressed and made up like a whore. Striptease by Ophelia. (55)

The variety of the *Hamlet* tradition makes it difficult to generalise about the play's heritage, other than to make the obvious point that the many attempts to rewrite the play are testimony to its ongoing vitality. I will, however, venture an additional generalisation. What we have seen in the heritage of *Hamlet* is the repeated impulse to simplify the complex character Shakespeare created. Romantics or moderns tend to seize on one side of Hamlet to the exclusion of the others. If Hegel's theory of tragedy is correct, this means that reinterpreters of Hamlet in effect lose sight of precisely what makes him tragic. Shakespeare's Hamlet is subject to despair and has an acute sense of the futility of heroic endeavour. But if that were the sum total of Hamlet's character, he would not be a tragic figure. If he did not simultaneously respond to man's potential for heroism, he would not experience such a bitter self-division, which in many ways is at the heart of his paralysis of will.

If studying the heritage of *Hamlet* teaches us anything, it is that each age has had its characteristic insights into the play but also its characteristic blind spots. It is of course notoriously difficult to see one's own blind spot, but it seems to me that what the modern era is most in danger of missing when it looks at *Hamlet* is the heroic dimension of the play. Our age is profoundly skeptical of heroism, especially of the conventional forms of military and aristocratic heroism which so often stand at the centre of Shakespeare's tragedies. As a result, ironic rereadings of plays like *Hamlet* are the fashion at the moment, both from critics analysing the play and creative writers attempting in one form or another to rework it (not to mention directors trying to stage it). But as I have argued, if we lose sight of what makes Hamlet heroic, we lose sight of what makes his story tragic. It is then in the spirit of antithetical criticism that I have tried in this book to restore a sense of what makes Hamlet unique as a hero and indeed what makes him uniquely heroic.

Works cited

Auerbach, Erich, *Mimesis: The Representation of Reality in Western Literature*, trans. Willard Trask (Princeton, 1953)

Barth, John, *The End of the Road* (New York, 1969)

Bullough, Geoffrey, ed., *Narrative and Dramatic Sources of Shakespeare* (London, 1973)

de Camoens, Luis, *The Lusiads*, trans. Leonard Bacon (New York, 1950)

Cavafy, C. P., *The Complete Poems*, trans. Rae Dalven (New York, 1976)

Coleridge, Samuel Taylor, *Shakespeare Criticism*, ed. Thomas Middleton Raysor (London, 1960)

Erasmus, Desiderius, 'Convivium Religiosum', in *Opera Omnia* (Amsterdam, 1972), Vol. III

The Education of a Christian Prince, trans. Leonard K. Born (New York, 1939)

von Goethe, Johann Wolfgang, *Wilhelm Meister's Apprenticeship*, trans. Thomas Carlyle (New York, 1959)

Hazlitt, William, *Characters of Shakespeare's Plays* (1817; rpt London, 1955)

Heinemann, Margot, 'How Brecht read Shakespeare', in Jonathan Dollimore and Alan Sinfield, eds., *Political Shakespeare* (Ithaca, New York, 1985)

Homer, *The Iliad*, trans. Richmond Lattimore (Chicago, 1951)

Jenkins, Harold, ed., *Hamlet* (London, 1982)

Johnson, Samuel, *The Works of Samuel Johnson* (New Haven, 1968)

Jones, Ernest, *Hamlet and Oedipus* (New York, 1949)

Kyd, Thomas, *The Spanish Tragedy*, ed. J. R. Mulryne (London, 1970)

Lukács, Georg, *The Historical Novel*, trans. Hannah and Stanley Mitchell (Lincoln, Nebraska, 1983)

McGinn, Donald Joseph, *Shakespeare's Influence on the Drama of his Age: Studied in Hamlet* (New Brunswick, New Jersey, 1938)

Machiavelli, Niccolò, *The Prince and the Discourses*, trans. Christian E. Detmold (New York, 1950)

Marlowe, Christopher, *The Complete Plays*, ed. J. B. Steane (Harmondsworth, 1969)

Marston, John, *Antonio's Revenge*, ed. G. K. Hunter (Lincoln, 1965)

Massinger, Philip, *The Selected Plays of Philip Massinger*, ed. Colin Gibson (Cambridge, 1978)

Milton, John, *Paradise Lost*, ed. Merritt Y. Hughes (New York, 1935)

Müller, Heiner, *Hamletmachine and Other Texts for the Stage*, trans. Carl Weber (New York, 1984)

Nietzsche, Friedrich, *Beyond Good and Evil*, trans. Walter Kaufmann (New York, 1966)

  The Will to Power, trans. Walter Kaufmann and R. J. Hollingdale (New York, 1967)

Rabelais, François, *Gargantua and Pantagruel*, trans. Jacques LeClerq (New York, 1942)

Scofield, Martin, *The Ghosts of Hamlet: The Play and Modern Writers* (Cambridge, 1980)

Stoppard, Tom, *Dogg's Hamlet, Cahoot's Macbeth* (London, 1980)

  Rosencrantz and Guildenstern Are Dead (New York, 1967)

Tourneur, Cyril, *The Plays of Cyril Tourneur*, ed. George Parfitt (Cambridge, 1978)

Wells, Stanley, ed., *Nineteenth-Century Shakespeare Burlesques* (London, 1977)

Guide to further reading

Background

For readers interested in a general view of the Renaissance, Jacob Burckhardt's classic *The Civilisation of the Renaissance in Italy* (Basel, 1860) remains the best introduction. A good collection of essays reflecting the debate on the Renaissance Burkhardt inaugurated can be found in Karl H. Donnenfeldt, ed., *The Renaissance: Medieval or Modern?* (Boston, 1959). For the history of the idea of the Renaissance, see Wallace K. Ferguson, *The Renaissance in Historical Thought* (Cambridge, Mass., 1948).

For readers interested in the theory of tragedy, Hegel's writings on the subject have been conveniently collected in Anne and Henry Paolucci, eds., *Hegel on Tragedy* (New York, 1962). This volume also contains A. C. Bradley's helpful essay, 'Hegel's Theory of Tragedy', originally published in Bradley's *Oxford Lectures on Poetry* (London, 1909). A superior translation of the sections on tragedy in Hegel's *Aesthetics* is now available in T. M. Knox's complete edition (Oxford, 1975).

Of the many books on English Renaissance drama, I would particularly recommend three. For a comprehensive survey of the revenge play background to *Hamlet*, see Fredson T. Bowers, *Elizabethan Revenge Tragedy, 1587–1642* (Princeton, 1940). Among recent studies which call into question the traditional Christian humanist readings of Renaissance drama, I would especially recommend for its clarity and forthrightness Jonathan Dollimore, *Radical Tragedy: Religion, Ideology and Power in the Drama of Shakespeare and his Contemporaries* (Sussex, 1984). For an important reinterpretation of Renaissance drama – one which stresses the significance of the classical tradition – see Gordon Braden, *Renaissance Tragedy and the Senecan Tradition* (New Haven, 1985), a book which builds up to a tantalisingly brief but powerfully suggestive discussion of *Hamlet*.

For biographical information on Shakespeare, see Samuel Schoenbaum, *William Shakespeare: A Documentary Life* (New York, 1975). Among the many excellent critical studies on Shakespeare to appear in recent years, I would single out A. D. Nuttall, *A New Mimesis: Shakespeare and the Representation of Reality* (London, 1983) and Harriett Hawkins, *The Devil's Party: Critical*

Counter-Interpretations of Shakespearian Drama (Oxford, 1985). The Hawkins book contains an excellent attack on mistaken moralistic criticism of *Hamlet*; though the Nuttall book does not discuss *Hamlet* in detail, it provides a welcome corrective to the excesses of much recent Shakespeare criticism and an epistemological justification for the approach I have taken in this book of treating *Hamlet* as a serious representation of Renaissance reality. For a brief but insightful discussion of Shakespearean tragedy in relation to the classical and the Christian traditions, see Walter Kaufmann, 'Shakespeare: Between Socrates and Existentialism', in his *From Shakespeare to Existentialism* (Garden City, New York, 1960).

Hamlet

More has been written about *Hamlet* than any other single work of literature, and I cannot pretend to have read more than a fraction of this vast body of criticism. What follows is therefore necessarily a personal set of recommendations: these are the studies of *Hamlet* which I have found most interesting and illuminating, and which have shaped my understanding of the play. I have made a special effort to call attention to little-known and out-of-the way writings on *Hamlet* which I believe are unjustly neglected.

Of the many scholarly editions of *Hamlet*, probably the most useful single volume is the one in the Arden Shakespeare series, edited by Harold Jenkins (already listed under Works cited). Jenkins provides a comprehensive and lucid summary of the current state of scholarship concerning *Hamlet*, dealing with such matters as its date, its sources and the various texts of the play. Readers interested in consulting facsimile reproductions of the original texts can find the First and Second Quartos in Michael J. B. Allen and Kenneth Muir, eds., *Shakespeare's Plays in Quarto* (Berkeley, California, 1981) and the First Folio text in Charlton Hinman, ed., *The First Folio of Shakespeare* (New York, 1968). The sources and analogues of *Hamlet*, including translations of Saxo, Belleforest and *Der bestrafte Brudermord*, are conveniently collected in Bullough, Vol. VII (listed under Works cited).

Among the classic interpretations of *Hamlet*, A. C. Bradley's in his *Shakespearean Tragedy* (London, 1904) remains an indispensable introduction to study of the play, in part because it sums up all of the nineteenth century's work on *Hamlet*, in part because it demonstrates such insight into the play. Among more recent studies, three stand out in my view, especially for their serious attempt to come to terms with *Hamlet* in light of the heroic tradition: Reuben A. Brower's chapter, 'Hamlet Hero', in his *Hero and Saint: Shakespeare and the Graeco-Roman Heroic Tradition* (Oxford, 1971); Anne Barton's introduction to T. J. B. Spencer's edition of

Hamlet (Harmondsworth, 1980); and G. K. Hunter's 'The Heroism of Hamlet', in John Russell Brown and Bernard Harris, eds., *Hamlet* (London, 1963). The Brown and Harris volume is one of the best collections of essays on *Hamlet*, including an illuminating essay by E. A. J. Honigmann on 'The Politics in *Hamlet* and "The World of the Play" '. Another useful collection of essays on the play is David Bevington, ed., *Twentieth Century Interpretations of Hamlet* (Englewood Cliffs, New Jersey, 1968), which includes Maynard Mack's well-known essay, 'The World of *Hamlet*'.

For other approaches to *Hamlet*, and more specialised topics, I can offer only a brief sample. For the classic psychoanalytic approach, see Ernest Jones's book (listed under Works cited). For a more humane and expansive Freudian discussion of the play, see Arthur Kirsch, 'Hamlet's Grief', *ELH* 48 (1981) 17–36, an essay which discusses *Hamlet* in terms of Freud's ideas on mourning and melancholia, rather than the Oedipus complex. For another psychoanalytic approach, see Anna K. Nardo, 'Hamlet, "A Man to Double Business Bound" ', *Shakespeare Quarterly* 34 (1983) 181–99. For an essay which criticises the Freudian approach to *Hamlet*, see René Girard, 'Hamlet's Dull Revenge', in Patricia Parker and David Quint, eds., *Literary Theory/Renaissance Texts* (Baltimore, 1986). This essay, which applies Girard's fascinating theory of mimetic desire to *Hamlet*, is important as one of the few sustained efforts to view *Hamlet* as an anti-revenge play; it does an excellent job of bringing out the tension between Christianity and the revenge ethic.

For Marxist analyses of *Hamlet*, see A. A. Smirnov, *Shakespeare: A Marxist Interpretation*, trans. Sonia Volochova (New York, 1936) and Thomas Metscher, 'Shakespeare in the Context of Renaissance Europe', *Science and Society* 41 (1977) 17–24. For a critique of historicist readings of *Hamlet*, see Helen Gardner's 'The Historical Approach' in her *The Business of Criticism* (Oxford, 1959). For one of the best and most compact discussions of the poetic imagery of *Hamlet* – a kind of New Critical reading of the play – see the chapter in Derek Traversi's *An Approach to Shakespeare* (Garden City, New York, 1969). Mark Rose has an instructive discussion of the structure of *Hamlet* in the chapter 'The Design of *Hamlet*' in his *Shakespearean Design* (Cambridge, Mass., 1972). For an interesting discussion of the central scenes of *Hamlet*, see Maurice Charney, 'The "Now Could I Drink Hot Blood" Soliloquy and the Middle of *Hamlet*', *Mosaic* 10 (1977) 77–86.

For discussions of the issue of symbolic geography in *Hamlet*, see Keith Brown, 'Hamlet's Place on the Map', *Shakespeare Studies* 4 (1969) 160–82; Gunnar Sjögren, 'The Geography of *Hamlet*', in his *Hamlet the Dane* (Lund, Sweden, 1983); Joan H. Landis, 'Shakespeare's Poland', *Hamlet Studies* 6 (1984) 8–17; and Vincent

F. Petronella, '*Hamlet*: The International Theme', *Hamlet Studies* 6 (1984) 18–29. For background on fencing in *Hamlet*, see S. P. Zitner, 'Hamlet, Duellist', *University of Toronto Quarterly* 39 (1969) 1–18.